Reviews and Advances in Fintech I

Global Fintech Institute - World Scientific Series on Fintech

Print ISSN: 2737-5897
Online ISSN: 2737-5900

In the digital era, emerging technologies such as artificial intelligence, big data, and blockchain have revolutionized people's daily lives and brought many opportunities and challenges to industries. With the increasing demand for talents in the fintech realm, this book series serves as a good guide for practitioners who are seeking to understand the basics of fintech and the applications of different technologies. This book series starts with fundamental knowledge in finance, technology, quantitative methods, and financial innovation to lay the foundation for the fundamentals of fintech, and understanding the trending issues related to fintech such as regulation, applications, and global trends. It is a good starting point to the fintech literature and is especially useful for people who aspire to become fintech professionals.

Published:

Vol. 6 *Reviews and Advances in Fintech I*
edited by David LEE Kuo Chuen, Daniel LIEBAU and Cindy DENG Xin

Vol. 5 *Applications and Trends in Fintech II: Cloud Computing, Compliance, and Global Fintech Trends*
edited by David LEE Kuo Chuen, Joseph LIM, PHOON Kok Fai and WANG Yu

Vol. 4 *Applications and Trends in Fintech I: Governance, AI, and Blockchain Design Thinking*
edited by David LEE Kuo Chuen, Joseph LIM, PHOON Kok Fai and WANG Yu

Vol. 3 *Fintech for Finance Professionals*
edited by David LEE Kuo Chuen, Joseph LIM, PHOON Kok Fai and WANG Yu

Vol. 2 *Finance for Fintech Professionals*
edited by David LEE Kuo Chuen, Joseph LIM, PHOON Kok Fai and WANG Yu

Vol. 1 *Foundations for Fintech*
edited by David LEE Kuo Chuen, Joseph LIM, PHOON Kok Fai and WANG Yu

More information on this series can also be found at https://www.worldscientific.com/series/gfiwssf

Global Fintech Institute - World Scientific Series on Fintech 6

Reviews and Advances in Fintech I

Editors

David LEE Kuo Chuen
Singapore University of Social Sciences, Singapore

Daniel LIEBAU
Singapore Management University, Singapore

Cindy DENG Xin
Nanyang Technological University, Singapore

Global Fintech Institute CFtP World Scientific

Published by

World Scientific Publishing Co. Pte. Ltd.
5 Toh Tuck Link, Singapore 596224
USA office: 27 Warren Street, Suite 401-402, Hackensack, NJ 07601
UK office: 57 Shelton Street, Covent Garden, London WC2H 9HE

and

Global Fintech Institute Ltd.
80 Robinson Road, #08-01, Singapore 068898

British Library Cataloguing-in-Publication Data
A catalogue record for this book is available from the British Library.

Global Fintech Institute - World Scientific Series on Fintech — Vol. 6
REVIEWS AND ADVANCES IN FINTECH I

ISBN 978-981-98-0674-4 (hardcover)
ISBN 978-981-98-0675-1 (ebook for institutions)
ISBN 978-981-98-0676-8 (ebook for individuals)

For any available supplementary material, please visit
https://www.worldscientific.com/worldscibooks/10.1142/14147#t=suppl

Desk Editor: Jiang Yulin

Typeset by Stallion Press
Email: enquiries@stallionpress.com

Foreword

As we navigate the rapidly evolving landscape of Fintech and blockchain, bold leadership is essential to unlocking the full potential. However, if you are a leader looking for a step-by-step guide to implementing the latest advances in Fintech and blockchain, this is not the book for you! *Reviews and Advances in Fintech I* is for you if you are the kind of leader who knows how to take calculated risks and seeks current knowledge to support decisions. It is also an essential book for leaders who seek clarity on what we know and still need to learn about the emerging world of blockchain and decentralized finance.

Reviews and Advances in Fintech I is an edited volume based on the first issue of World Scientific's *Annual Review of Fintech Journal*. It contains the original five journal articles, which have been enhanced by current commentaries. The book also features four contributions by industry experts, covering recent Fintech developments.

It has been a privilege to write this foreword to add my insights on the leadership necessary to propel Fintech forward, drawn from my nearly three decades of leadership and transformation experience in financial services and my advanced studies in leadership at the master's level.

After reading the book, one thing is clear: Fintech, DeFi and blockchain solutions are gaining greater traction in finance. One could argue that articles created in 2023 are already outdated, but I would challenge that assumption. While the learning will never stop, practitioners will benefit from this book not only because the core articles can assist them in understanding the fundamentals and how solutions were developed but also because from the updated commentary and insights into the industry, they can assess the trends that have emerged since. The book provides an essential grounding that will remain relevant for years to come in addressing the potential weakness of many DeFi teams, who, in their rush to disrupt traditional finance, may have forgotten to learn and mitigate critical lessons from TradFi.

Embracing learning from past failures is an essential leadership skill. The book will serve those who seek a clearer understanding of how Fintech solutions can fail. What struck me the most as I read all five of the core articles was that each limitation described is a failing of humans not code. This human impact suggests that now is the time for strong leadership to overcome the obstacles that currently stand in the way of blockchain and Fintech solutions fully integrating into the traditional world of finance.

As an organizational psychologist who examines the intersection between companies and humans, I found the article "A Survey of Decentralized Autonomous Organizations (DAOs) and Their Governance" fascinating. Having studied how humans add unnecessary bureaucratic complexity to processes, DAOs invoked, to me, a utopian vision of replacing this with rules captured and executed by code. The prospect of automated controls is exciting for the speed of execution possibilities it brings, which already benefits the c.$90 billion currently allocated to DeFi platforms. However, the cited studies revealed the need for complex governance processes to establish trust and mitigate the human tendency to circumnavigate controls and strive for power. The solutions DAOs implement often recreate the power imbalance inherent in our traditional organizations by limiting who can propose and vote for changes to the automated rules, frequently favoring the wealthy or power-hungry. The findings from the 1971 Stanford Prison Experiment, which studied how people's behavior changes depending on their situation, may apply here. Are those designing the DAO governance systems akin to the students appointed as prison guards who then abused their newfound power in less than six days? It will require a different leadership mindset to implement minimum viable governance processes if DAOs are to stay true to their decentralized ideal. The industry contribution "Privacy and New Types of Money" builds on this narrative, discussing the nuanced approach needed to balance privacy with control as blockchain finance moves into the mainstream of central and core banking.

The article "Building a Sustainable Future: Exploring Green Finance, Regenerative Finance, and Green Financial Technology" outlines the potential benefits that Fintech financing and blockchain-based tracking of sustainability goals could bring to humans and the planet through its insight into the currently known use cases. These insights beg the question: While most of the power still resides within the traditional finance world, rarely known for its altruistic nature, what might it take to make this systemic shift toward transparency?

The shift toward transparency and improved financing for sustainable initiatives may only come when sustainability leaders can tell compelling stories, build trust from the masses and put systemic pressure on traditional investment intermediaries. Yet, while the advocacy of technology to advance sustainability goals comes only from dissident tech and conservationist voices, it is easy for politicians and business leaders who focus on profits at all costs and fund managers who continue to invest in companies with high CO_2 emissions to ignore. Public trust in the ESG initiatives of many traditional businesses is low as rumors of greenwashing abound, a challenge that blockchain-based tracking could address. However, a systemic shift to full transparency typically requires regulation to drive behavior change. My concern is that while regulators are busy mitigating the risks of traditional finance, the need to drive genuinely sustainable finance may only become a priority when it is already too late. Does Greentech need its own leader, *à la* Henry Ford, Elon Musk, or Whitney Wolfe Herd, to shake up the status quo and bring transparent blockchain-based sustainable investments into the mainstream? Perhaps, that leader is you?

It could be easy to assume that DeFi may still fail due to a lack of adoption, but the industry contribution "NFTs: Hype, Hope or Here to Stay?" provides a glimmer of hope. It outlines how, once thought almost worthless, NFTs have recently ignited new possibilities in the real-world assets space, including stocks, real estate, and luxury items.

In the article "An In-depth Guide to Cross-chain Protocols under a Multi-chain World", we learn about the necessity of integration if any blockchain-based solution is to be scalable, trustworthy and resilient enough to support mainstream finance. The article lays out the known architectures alongside their limitations. Once again, a limiting factor is the human inability to collaborate and put aside personal interests for the benefit of the consumer and the greater good. Achieving cross-chain collaboration at a global scale would require several key players to work together, possibly abandoning their solutions in favor of a common protocol. We have accomplished similar feats through the SWIFT network and even the standardization of USB-C chargers. Still, it takes strong vision and leadership to create alignment and drive the agenda for a change of this scale. The industry contribution "Intermediaries in the Age of a Decentralized Finternet" provides exciting insight into where that leadership may come from and how this new digital ecosystem could unite the finance world. The author also highlights the challenges and opportunities the Finternet brings to the wide network of intermediaries who run the current system.

"Voting Schemes in DAO Governance" sets another great leadership example. The article's authors have reviewed the known voting schemes and, acknowledging the limitations of each, applied design thinking for a more comprehensive problem-solving approach. The focus is on deep understanding to ensure that they solve the right problem before designing an effective solution. Will the researchers' example inspire more Fintech leaders to consult diverse stakeholders to clearly define the problem before jumping to solutions?

The industry contribution "Counterparty Risk in DeFi" also calls for including more traditional finance skill sets to create integrated solutions with better outcomes for more people and mitigate the human and systemic counterparty risks that the author highlights still exist within decentralized finance.

The article "A Case Study of Ant Finance's Innovation Journey — From a Platform Economy Perspective" provides insight into how Jack Ma, a tech-savvy leader, disrupted traditional finance through the Ant Financial platform. Ant rewrote the market rules, using technology to provide low-risk credit to the previously unbanked. Perhaps, one of Jack Ma's most significant leadership challenges was identifying and aligning key stakeholders. Underestimating the Chinese Government's power and failing to keep it onside resulted in the last-minute cancellation of the much-anticipated IPO and invoked layers of new regulations. Despite this, the Ant Finance platform has grown and remains a beacon of Fintech success. This article provides several critical insights, including a framework to understand how Fintech platforms and ecosystems can evolve.

When viewing the book's content through the seminal lens of E.M. Rogers' *Diffusion of Innovation Curve Theory* (1962), we are already past the Innovators stage and into the Early Adopters phase.

If humans are to maximize blockchain's potential of DAOs, Greentech, Cross-Chain Collaboration, the Finternet and beyond, now is the time for bold leadership:

- Bold enough to move beyond the 'rebels against the establishment' origins of DeFi's creators. Their vision of transparency and eliminating privileged executives' control may fuel mistrust amongst the traditional financial and political leaders who hold the power to limit its adoption.
- Bold enough to embrace learning from how current solutions are failing.
- Bold enough to learn from the past and reassure leaders and employees that while technology changes people's work, it has never made us humans irrelevant and always drives us forward.
- Bold enough to tell a compelling story, educate and gain alignment from less tech-savvy leaders and help them discover their WIIFM (What Is In It For Me). We all must understand, demystify and remove the fear that blockchain and DeFi solutions provoke.

Only when leaders embrace fintech solutions and move them into the core of finance can we tap into the critical mass of Roger's 'Early Majority' required to integrate, sustain, and realize the massive possibility and potential revealed by this book.

I hope that *Reviews and Advances in Fintech I* will support and inspire you as you determine the part you will play.

Leah Stockley
MSc Org. Psych. and Co-Founder of Lets Flow.sg

Reference

Rogers, E. M., 1962, *Diffusion of Innovations.* Free Press of Glencoe.

About the Editors

David LEE Kuo Chuen is a Professor of Fintech and Blockchain at the Singapore University of Social Sciences (SUSS), a Distinguished Professor at Shanghai University of Finance and Economics, an Adjunct Professor at the National University of Singapore (NUS), a founding Council Member of the British Blockchain Association, and Editor-in-Chief or Deputy Editor-in-Chief of the *Journal of Fintech* and *Annual Review of Fintech*.

Meanwhile, Professor Lee is also an internationally renowned scholar and industry opinion leader in the field of blockchain, an expert in the development of Web3 and Artificial Intelligence (AI) application scenarios, the Chairman of the Global FinTech Institute (GFI), a co-founder of the Singapore Blockchain Association, a co-founder of the Blockchain Security Alliance and Global Web3 Association, a CBDC advisor to the Asian Development Bank, Vice President of the Economic Society of Singapore (ESS), a cryptocurrency advisor to the Asian Institute of Digital Finance (AIDF) of NUS, an advisor to the SUSS Node for inclusive FinTech (NiFT), an independent director of several listed companies in Singapore, an angel investor in blockchain, Web3, inclusive finance and AI innovation, a senior advisor and Investment Committee member of Artichoke Capital which is backed by institutional limited partners, including sovereign wealth and family office funds.

Professor Lee previously served as a Senior Advisor to the Provost of Singapore Management University (SMU), Director of the Sim Kee Boon Institute for Financial Economic (SKBI) in Singapore, a member of the Research Council of the Monetary Authority of Singapore (MAS), a member of the Technical Advisory Committee of Ping An OneConnect, an independent director of Lu Global in Singapore, and long taught at the Mayor's Class in Singapore. In addition, Professor Lee served as an international consultant to the Distributed Trust Research Project at Stanford University, Group MD of listed companies OUE Enterprise and Auric Pacific, a Fellow at Harvard University–National

University of Singapore (1991–1993), a Fulbright Scholar at Stanford University in 2015, the founder of hedge fund Ferrell Asset Management, and the founder of real estate developer Ferrell Residences.

Xin (Cindy) DENG is an Associate Professor of Finance (Practice), Assistant Dean of ASEAN and China Programmes and Co-Director of the Centre for Sustainable Finance and Innovation (CSFI) at Nanyang Business School, Nanyang Technological University. She is the CFA charter holder and serves as the Chief FinTech Expert at the Shanghai International Financial Centre Research Institute and the Academic Committee member of the Global FinTech Institute. She has published in leading finance and management journals such as *Journal of Financial Economics*, *Strategic Management Journal*, *Journal of Financial and Quantitative Analysis*, *Journal of Banking and Finance*, etc. She is a highly cited Chinese scholar by Elsevier.

Daniel (Dan) LIEBAU is a pracademic: As a practitioner, he is Founder of Lightbulb Capital in Hong Kong and Singapore. Previously, Dan was the CIO of the Modular Blockchain Fund at Modular Asset Management and the COO of HSBC Securities in Singapore. As an academic, he is an Affiliate Faculty Member at Singapore Management University where he teaches courses on Blockchain & Digital Assets, and Decentralized Finance (DeFi). He is also a Lecturer in ESSEC's top-ranked Master in Finance program. Previously he was a visiting professor at IE business school, where he received the teaching excellence award. His research work investigates blockchain in the financial markets context has been published by various academic journals by Springer and MIT Press. He is also the Associate Editor-in-Chief of *World Scientific Annual Review of Fintech* journal. Dan is completing his PhD in Finance at Erasmus University, and holds Master degrees in Innovation (SMU) and Finance (IE).

About the Contributors

Kenneth Bok is Managing Director of Blocks.sg, a DeFi advisory firm based in Singapore, and author of *Decentralizing Finance*. Previously, Kenneth served as Head of Growth and Strategy at Zilliqa, a blockchain technology company, where he led ecosystem and business development. Kenneth is also a pro-bono mentor for R3.

Kenneth began his career in finance as an equities trader at Goldman Sachs. Since 2014, he has been an investor in digital assets, particularly 'Layer 1' blockchains such as Ethereum. He holds an M.Eng. in Mechanical Engineering from Imperial College and an M.A. in Philosophy from CIIS.

Alvin Chia is Head of Digital Assets Innovation for Asia Pacific at Northern Trust. He is responsible for developing market-leading innovations aligned with Northern Trust's digital asset strategy. Alvin drives Northern Trust's interactions with Fintechs, industry bodies, regulators and government to positively influence market change in line with the organisation's strategic direction.

Alvin brings more than 10 years of experience in various innovation-related roles. Most recently, he was the Expert Senior Manager of Innovation at Bain and Company, where he helped senior leaders from Fortune 500 companies achieve their strategic ambitions. Prior to Bain, Alvin served as the Vice President of Innovation at DBS Bank, where he co-created numerous flagship digital products and services for the bank across Asia.

Alvin is an alumnus of the National University of Singapore (NUS), Nanyang Technological University, and is currently completing a doctoral degree in digital innovation at NUS.

Luc Froehlich is Chief Commercial Officer at RAK DAO, a free zone dedicated to digital asset companies, and the former Global Head of Digital Assets Solutions at Fidelity International. Along with his role at Fidelity, Luc has authored research with the World Economic Forum on distributed ledger technology in capital markets, central bank digital currencies and cryptocurrencies.

Before joining Fidelity, Luc was a portfolio manager, managing money for central banks and pension funds; he was a proprietary trader in credit derivatives and started his career as a credit analyst.

Luc holds a Master's degree in Economics and Business Administration from the University of St. Gallen, Switzerland, a Master of Science in Blockchain and Digital Currency from the University of Nicosia, Cyprus, and he is a CFA and CAIA charterholder. Since 2017, he has been advising start-ups leading financial innovation, particularly blockchain-based, and guest lecturing on digital assets at several universities.

Sandy Oh is an Associate Instructor and Advisor to Lightbulb Capital, a Singapore- and Hong Kong-based firm that collaborates with members of the financial industry to learn and adopt transformational technology. Through Singapore Management University's Academy, Sandy teaches classes on blockchain, digital assets, and Non-Fungible Tokens (NFTs). Prior to discovering blockchain and its myriad applications, Sandy held senior fixed income sales roles in HSBC, Jefferies, ING, Commerzbank and J.P Morgan. She has an MBA from University of Chicago Booth School of Business and a BA in Politics, Philosophy and Economics from Oxford University.

Editorial Note
Welcome to the Annual Review of Fintech

We welcome you to the *Annual Review of Fintech* (*WSARFT*). The journey to establish this journal was not without its challenges. Still, we are proud to have overcome them and bring you this unique publication.

Several significant milestones marked the road to the launch of the *Annual Review of Fintech*. We encountered many hurdles, from the initial discussions between World Scientific (WS) and the Global Fintech Institute (GFI) to the painstaking process of selecting the right editorial team. However, through hard work, sometimes at late hours, we overcame these obstacles and set up a journal that we believe will have a significant impact.

A bit of history: Approximately 18 months ago, World Scientific approached David to become the Editor-in-Chief of a new journal dedicated to Fintech. The publisher had recently launched the *Journal of Fintech*, our sister journal, and recognized the potential for further exploration in this field. To complement the primary academic research focus of the *Journal of Fintech*, a premier publication for the GFI that oversees the administration of the Chartered Fintech Professionals qualifications, WS and GFI have partnered to launch this new publication, the *Annual Review of Fintech*. The objective of the new journal was to establish a leading outlet for review papers that survey the literature on Fintech, summarizing the trends and novel phenomena reshaping finance. As part of its commitment to fostering continuous education and professional development, GFI intends to include selected articles from journals both in the educational materials for Chartered Fintech Professionals and other educational programs. By providing access to cutting-edge research and insights, GFI is helping to equip the next generation of Fintech professionals with the skills and knowledge they need to succeed in this rapidly evolving industry.

David, in turn, approached Cindy and Daniel to become Associate Editors-in-Chief. We believe we have complementary skills, including extensive academic and industry experience, top-tier journal publications, and a broad network of prospective Associate Editors. We also shared a passion for Fintech, a critical characteristic for the startup-like endeavor.

With the core team in place, we designed the review process and assembled an experienced advisory board. Cam Harvey of Duke University and David Yermack of NYU Stern, both highly cited researchers with excellent publications, accepted the invitations to join. Will Cong of Cornell, a leading finance/econ researcher investigating blockchain systems, later joined the board. The support of the advisory board is very much appreciated as they boost the team's confidence.

Selecting Associate Editors proved challenging. We sought a mix of skills, backgrounds, and genders from diverse geographical locations. However, we discovered that Fintech research is nascent, and only few scholars tick all the boxes. Eventually, we assembled a unique group, including scholars from France, Chile, the United States, the Netherlands, Australia, and China.

Despite progress, we faced a significant hurdle in attracting quality review paper submissions. The fast-moving nature of the Fintech field and limited research in some areas made it challenging to identify suitable articles to survey. Additionally, as a new journal with no track record or indexing, we also faced challenges in attracting submissions. Nonetheless, we persisted, contacting authors with interesting draft papers on SSRN and arXiv.

In the spirit of entrepreneurship, we recognized the need to bootstrap for the first issue. David's guidance was critical in setting realistic expectations for the journal's establishment and recognizing the need to start somewhere, even if that meant accepting reviews of recent developments in the market alongside pure academic review papers.

Next, we would like to take this opportunity to thank everyone who played a role in bringing the *Annual Review of Fintech* to life. From our authors and reviewers to our editorial team and support staff, we are grateful for your contributions and dedication. We hope this journal will serve as a platform for exchanging ideas and insights that will help shape the future of the Fintech industry. We want to thank our colleagues at World Scientific, particularly Jiang Yulin, for his relentless management of our editorial team. We also thank our Associate Editors for their willingness to embark on an entrepreneurial journey of starting a new journal with us. We also extend our appreciation to our advisory board for their guidance, networks, and practical advice. Their contributions have been invaluable in the success of the *Annual Review of Fintech*. We are excited to present this first issue to you and look forward to sharing many more significant publications in the future. We hope you find this journal informative, engaging, and thought-provoking.

We are pleased to present an eclectic mix of articles showcasing the latest developments and research in Fintech. While we do not yet have submissions from Nobel Prize winners or scholars who typically publish in top-tier journals, we are confident that our journal's reputation will grow over time. We will attract even more high-quality contributions.

Next, we would like to introduce the articles selected for our first issue. The first article, "A Survey on Decentralized Autonomous Organizations (DAOs) and Their Governance", authored by Qinxu Ding, Zhiguo Wang, and Weibiao Xu of the Singapore University of Social Sciences (SUSS), and our Editor, Daniel Liebau of the Rotterdam School of Management at the Erasmus University in the Netherlands, offers a comprehensive overview of DAOs and their governance. The article provides a helpful framework for understanding the fundamental characteristics of DAOs and discusses the challenges of resolving disputes. The authors' insights are valuable to novice researchers and practitioners interested in DAOs. The article also provides some research ideas in this developing field.

Another article in this issue is titled "Building a Sustainable Future: Exploring Green Finance, Regenerative Finance, and Green Financial Technology", which examines the role of green technology in meeting dual carbon goals. The author, Carmen Shih of the Singapore University of Social Sciences, our Editor, Cindy Deng of the Nanyang Technological University, and Andrzej Gwizdalski of the University of Western Australia discuss the significance of green technology in reducing carbon emissions and provide insights into the future potential of green technology to contribute to sustainable economic development.

The article "An In-depth Guide to Cross-Chain Protocols under a Multi-Chain World" offers a detailed analysis of cross-chain protocols in a multi-chain environment. The authors Jincheng Zheng of SUSS, our Editor David Lee, and Dejun Qian of Chainge Finance provide a comprehensive overview of the different cross-chain protocols and their applications, highlighting the benefits and challenges of each protocol with a case study.

The "Voting Schemes in DAO Governance" article by the SUSS team Qinxu Ding, Weibiao Xu, Zhiguo Wang, and David Lee examines different voting schemes and structures. The article highlights the importance of transparency and fairness in voting.

Finally, we are pleased to include a paper by Herve Alexandre, Professor at Paris Dauphine in France, and Kok Lian Woo, Associate Professor at Shenzhen

University in China, that discusses the platform economy using Chinese Fintech firm Ant as an example. It also highlights the problem that regulators find themselves in when wanting to protect the consumer, on the one hand, and aiming to foster innovation in the financial services industry, on the other.

We are confident these articles will provide relevant insights and contribute to the ongoing discourse on Fintech. We hope you find them informative and engaging and look forward to your feedback on our first issue. We know there is room for improvement. But we are also daring to kick-start and plan to develop continuously.

Now that you have gained insight into our journey and the first issue's publication, we are excited to highlight our plans. Our focus has shifted to the second issue, which will revolve around "Data Science and Marketing in Traditional and Decentralized Finance". As with the first issue, our goal is to contribute to advancing Fintech theory and practice. We will be issuing a formal call for papers shortly.

While we had to bootstrap for the first issue, we hope to leverage our experienced Associate Editors for the peer review process for the second issue. We encourage them to consider partnering with junior researchers in their departments to submit review papers. Review papers are an excellent starting point for Ph.D. students to gain a deeper understanding of their chosen literature and identify gaps in the field. Eventually, writing a review paper can assist them in focusing their research and subsequently closing out gaps documented in their initial work.

Review papers are crucial in advancing our understanding of Fintech, synthesizing existing knowledge and often becoming highly cited. Like theory and empirical papers, review papers are vital to advancing the field's understanding.

We also want to encourage global faculty members outside of our network to consider submitting their review papers with us. We welcome their contributions to our mission of contributing to the discourse.

The rapid advancement of technology in the Fintech industry has inevitably influenced academic research. In light of this, we welcome authors to use artificial intelligence (AI) in their research, provided that such usage is disclosed and does not infringe intellectual property rights. To this end, we will give the authors detailed guidelines on using AI-generated content and research, which we will continually update as necessary. As an example of using AI technology to enhance writing style, we have utilized ChatGPT to draft this Editorial. However, we emphasize that the contents and responsibilities of this Editorial remain entirely our own. We aim to ensure that AI's use in research is conducted ethically and transparently while also embracing the benefits of such technology in advancing our understanding of Fintech.

Kind regards from the editorial team of World Scientific's *Annual Review of Fintech* journal.

David Kuo Chuen Lee
Editor-in-Chief
Global Fintech Institute
Singapore 068898, Singapore
Singapore University of Social Sciences
Singapore 599494, Singapore
davidleekc@suss.edu.sg

Daniel Liebau
Associate Editor-in-Chief
Rotterdam School of Management, Erasmus University
3062 PA Rotterdam, The Netherlands
Singapore Management University
Singapore 188065, Singapore
liebau@rsm.nl

Xin Deng
Associate Editor-in-Chief
Nanyang Business School, Nanyang Technological University
Singapore 639798, Singapore
xin.deng@ntu.edu.sg

Contents

A Commentary on "A Survey on Decentralized Autonomous Organizations (DAOs) and Their Governance"

Daniel Liebau

Department of Finance at Rotterdam School of Management, Erasmus University, The Netherlands
liebau@rsm.nl

1. Introduction

The original article "A Survey on Decentralized Autonomous Organizations (DAOs) and Their Governance" by Ding *et al.* (2023) provides a comprehensive overview of the state of DAO research. However, given the rapid pace of innovation in this field, several noteworthy contributions have emerged since its publication. It is impossible to cover all articles, so for this commentary, I aim to add value by selecting those that, in my mind, offer distinct and relevant new insights. This commentary will explore the latest findings on decentralization, DAO success factors, incentives, and idiosyncratic DAO attacks. I conclude by showcasing an article containing many open questions and ideas for future research. With it, I aim to extend the value of the original survey and contribute to the ongoing scholarly conversation surrounding DAOs. A commentary of a review article does not stand alone — I encourage the interested reader to explore the topics in more depth by reading some of the articles mentioned here.

2. Review

A critical issue in the DAO world is the level of decentralization. Several researchers have quantified decentralization by using distinct measures, such as the concentration of voting rights amongst DAO members. Axelsen *et al.* (2022) propose a framework for assessing the decentralization of DAOs more holistically, an important factor in determining their regulatory status. The authors identify five key dimensions — Token-weighted voting, Infrastructure, Governance, Escalation, and Reputation (TIGER) — that contribute to a DAO's level of decentralization. I believe this more comprehensive approach is more potent than a single metric.

Empirical articles investigating DAOs are on the rise. For example, Bellavitis *et al.* (2022) show a surge in DAOs with registered activity since November 2019. Laturnus (2023) dives deeper and shows that greater participation — interestingly by the number of participants, not the number of governance tokens — is associated with superior performance in the financial markets of governance tokens. She also documents that the level of decentralization of a DAO only plays a minor role in the valuation of governance tokens. In surveying 50 DAO projects, Werbach *et al.* (2024) add to our understanding of incentives within a DAO and show that over 80% of respondents use financial incentives to encourage members to contribute.

In their most recent draft article, Heimbach *et al.* (2024) provide crucial insights into security threats to DAOs, significantly contributing to the literature investigating risks. The authors analyze past, theorized, and potential attacks on DAOs, categorizing the attack vectors into four categories: The first is bribing, where an attacker pays to change votes or acquire voting power without acquiring the underlying governance tokens. The second is token control, where the attacker takes possession of or already possesses a significant amount of governance tokens. The third is human–computer interaction, where attacks aim to manipulate the voting process through exploiting user-facing interfaces and applications, or human behaviors involved in the DAO's voting process. The fourth is code and protocol vulnerability, where attackers exploit code or logic vulnerabilities, either in the governance smart contracts or the protocols they are connected to.

3. Conclusion and Outlook

This commentary would not be complete without mentioning the multidisciplinarity of the large team around Joshua Tan *et al.* (2023). In their article, the authors outline the many open questions that still need thorough investigation through diverse lenses, such as computer science, economics, ethics, law, organizational science, political science, and philosophy. They ask relevant questions: How can a DAO deal with privacy-related issues such as "corporate espionage, protecting the confidentiality of individuals and communities served by the organization and enabling surprise product releases, and defending against other vulnerabilities?" "What best practices should DAOs learn from traditional corporate governance, and what best practices should they reject?" Particularly important is the following: "How can DAOs comply with the objectives and spirit of laws and regulations intended to combat illicit activities, while still retaining their distinctive features (e.g., pseudonymous or anonymous contributors)?"

I see plenty of research opportunities when looking at the current state of DAOs, for example, investigating technical aspects, such as the impact of vote delegation on the decentralization of DAOs. However, two pressing themes deserve our attention in particular. The first is the development of frameworks to understand a DAO's idiosyncratic risks that are largely unknown to the corporate governance literature because DAOs are smart contracts based on blockchain technology. The second is a much deeper understanding of the cryptographic mechanisms that power these systems.

A more profound understanding of risks and cryptography will benefit policymakers, regulators, and industry professionals, particularly in the financial services industry. It will enable them to assess DAOs more adequately and devise the next steps to broader-scale adoption. So, entrepreneurs, technologists, and researchers alike have much work to do.

References

Axelsen, H., Jensen, J., and Ross, O., 2022. When is a DAO decentralized? Complex systems informatics and modeling quarterly, *CSIMQ*. https://doi.org/10.7250/csimq.2022-31.04.

Bellavitis, C., Fisch, C., and Momtaz, P., 2022. The rise of decentralized autonomous organizations (DAOs): A first empirical glimpse. *Venture Capital*. https://www.tandfonline.com/doi/full/10.1080/13691066.2022.2116797.

Ding, Q., Liebau, D., Wang, W., and Xu, W., 2023. A Survey on Decentralized Autonomous Organizations (DAOs) and Their Governance. *World Scientific Annual Review of Fintech*. https://www.worldscientific.com/doi/epdf/10.1142/S281100482350001X.

Heimbach, L, Feichtinger, R., Fritsch, R., Vonlanthen, Y., and Wattenhofer, R., 2024. SoK: Attacks on DAOs. *Working paper*. https://tik-db.ee.ethz.ch/file/a1e786715291c85920d1babd980affb7.

Laturnus, V. 2023. The Economics of Decentralized Autonomous Organisations. *Working paper*. https://papers.ssrn.com/sol3/papers.cfm?abstract_id=4320196.

Tan, J., Merk, T., Hubbard, S., Oak, E., Pirovich, J., Rennie, E., Hoefer, R., Zargham, M., Potts, J., Berg, C., Youngblom, R., De Filippi, P., Frey, S., Strnad, J., Mannan, M., Nabben, K., Elrrifai, S., Hartnell, J., Hill, B., Maddox, A., Lim, W., South, T., Juels. A., and Boneh, D., 2023. Open Problems in DAOs. *Working paper.* https://arxiv.org/abs/2310.19201.

Werbach, K., De Filippi, P., Tan, J., and Pieters, G., 2024. Blockchain governance in the wild. *Cryptoeconomic Systems Journal.* https://cryptoeconomicsystems.pubpub.org/pub/blockchain-governance-wild/release/1.

A Survey on Decentralized Autonomous Organizations (DAOs) and Their Governance*

Qinxu Ding[†,§], Daniel Liebau[‡,¶], Zhiguo Wang[†,||] and Weibiao Xu[†,**]

[†]*Department of Finance, School of Business*
Singapore University of Social Sciences
Singapore 599494, Singapore
[‡]*SMU Academy, Singapore Management University*
60 Stamford Road, Level 4, Singapore 178900, Singapore
[§]*qinxuding@suss.edu.sg*
[¶]*liebau@rsm.nl*
[||]*zwang@suss.edu.sg*
[**]*weibiaoxu@suss.edu.sg*

Decentralized Autonomous Organizations or DAOs are organizations governed by a set of pre-defined rules programmed as source code in smart contracts. Once implemented, a DAO can automatically execute tasks, coordinate, and facilitate decentralized decision-making, without any central authority. This new and emerging paradigm is still under development and has not been researched much until today. To our knowledge, the literature still lacks a comprehensive survey discussing DAOs and DAO governance. We conduct a systematic review of common characteristics, a DAO categorization, real-world DAO applications, DAO governance including voting schemes and dispute resolution mechanisms in DAOs to provide an initial overview. We anticipate that our work can provide useful insights and references for researchers and industrial practitioners who wish to delve deeper into this nascent area.

[*]This Chapter was originally published in the *World Scientific Annual Review of Fintech*, Vol. 1, No. 1, doi: 10.1142/S281100482350001X.

[||]Corresponding author.

Keywords: Decentralized autonomous organizations (DAOs); DAO governance; voting scheme; dispute resolution.

1. Introduction

Blockchain technology has attracted more attention in recent years, and several blockchain-based applications have been created to benefit from the technologies' decentralization, transparency, and high security (Guo *et al.*, 2022). Blockchain technology (Lee, 2020) has emerged as a new paradigm for governance, including distributed tokenization (Lee *et al.*, 2021; Lee *et al.*, 2022; Atzori, 2015), smart contracts (Lo *et al.*, 2021), autonomous automation, and transparent processing or codification of trust (Rozas *et al.*, 2021). The potential of blockchain governance is expressed through decentralized autonomous organizations (DAOs) (El Faqir *et al.*, 2020; Hsieh *et al.*, 2018).

DAOs are autonomous organizations, governed by a set of pre-defined rules programmed as source code. Once implemented, such smart contracts can automatically execute tasks and facilitate decentralized decision-making like hiring new members, providing services, coordinating with other DAOs, and so on (De Filippi and Hassan, 2018; Wright and De Filippi, 2015). This new and emerging paradigm is still under development and has not been researched much yet. It is therefore essential to conduct a systematic review of the current state of affairs. To our knowledge, most of the existing literature has focused on the review of DAO development or DAO platforms while barely addressing DAO governance. In this paper, we aim to review DAO design, a DAO categorization, recent DAO developments, and focus our review on DAO governance. Two groups may find this work beneficial. The first group consists of industrial practitioners. Our paper provides a quick overview of the organizational design of DAOs, DAO governance, and may enable the reader to appreciate possible implications for technology, society, business, politics, and the economy. The second group is that of academic researchers who look for a starting point to explore the subject more deeply (Hassan and De Filippi, 2021).

1.1. *What is a DAO?*

Today, there is no consensus or unique definition of what a DAO is. For example, Luis Cuende, co-founder of the Aragon DAO platform defines it as "an internet-native entity with no central management which is regulated by a set of automatically enforceable rules on a public blockchain, and whose goal is to take a life of its own and incentivize people to achieve a shared common mission".[1] Another description in De Filippi and Hassan (2021) states that in a DAO the interaction of members (individuals or computers) is mediated by a blockchain application that is governed by a set of rules written into its source code. In De Filippi and Hassan (2018), DAOs are ascribed the ability to hire people autonomously, provide services, gain money for their own aims, own smart property, coordinate with other autonomous software, or facilitate cooperation among various parties. Singh and Kim (2019) define a DAO as an organization whose core functions are automated, and that can agree, without human intervention, to the rules and principles specified in code.

In contrast to today's most prominently used entity to organize for work, the firm, DAOs feature a decentralized structure, without CEOs or executives. All members of a DAO are bound by the rules programmed into the smart contract code. DAO operations are entirely transparent and global, whereas conventional companies' operations are often opaque, with only the organization privy to inner workings. Any alterations to a DAO must be approved through a voting process. Its outcomes are stored immutably on a public blockchain.

In this paper, we define a DAO as an organization that enables individuals with common goals to collaborate using a blockchain infrastructure to enforce a set of shared rules. Typically, the members of a DAO are anonymously registered, each with a unique address. Members would have purchased any amount of "governance tokens" linked to their address. These tokens are usually required for participation in the decision-making process. Decisions include determining how to use or allocate the common resources, for example, funds, in a DAO.

1.2. *Survey methodology*

Figure 1 summarizes our literature review approach, process, and outcomes. First, we conduct a comprehensive search on primary keywords "DAO" and/or "decentralized autonomous organization", in various databases, including Engineering Village, Science Direct, ABI/INFORMS Collection, BIOSIS Preview, SpringerLink, IEEE Xplore, SSRN, and Google Scholar. We use secondary keywords "DAO governance" and/or "governance" and/or "governance of DAOs" to further identify relevant papers for the analysis of DAO governance. We perform a cross-referenced search by reviewing titles in the reference list of identified papers. The selection of the data sources is mainly based on prevailing representative

[1] https://aragon.substack.com/p/aragon-project-updates-may-2020.

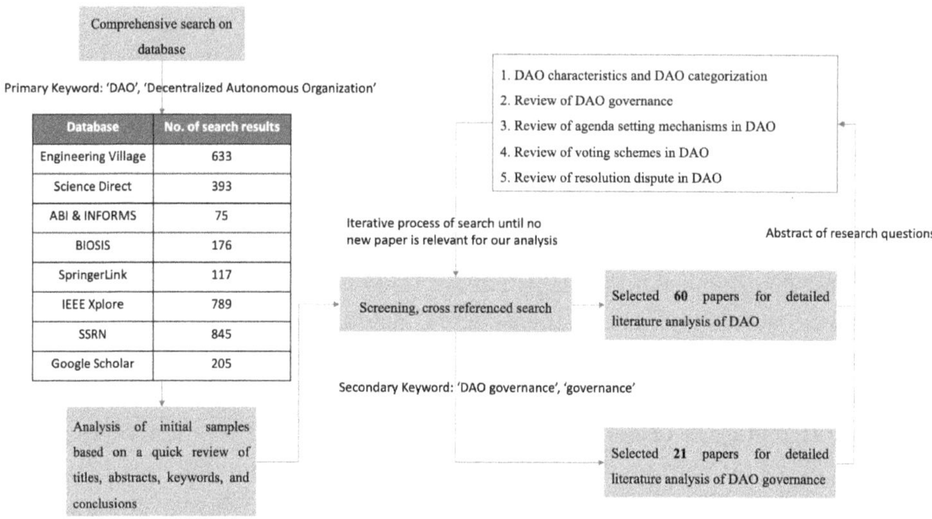

Fig. 1. Literature review process and outcome.

digital libraries for software engineering research (Liu *et al.*, 2021; Keele *et al.*, 2007), for the period between 2015 and 2022.

We also conduct a screening on the original sample (Liu *et al.*, 2021) and shortlist 60 DAO-related papers and 21 DAO governance papers, respectively, for further analysis. We review the titles, abstracts, keywords, and conclusions of the identified papers. We synthesize consistent insights from multiple articles by summarizing what we learn to give readers a sound introduction to the topic. We abstract the following five essential research questions from our review for a more detailed discussion in this paper.

1. What is a DAO? (DAO characteristics and categorization)
2. What is DAO governance?
3. What are the different agenda-setting mechanisms?
4. What are the different voting schemes in DAO?
5. Does dispute resolution work in DAOs?

The rest of this paper is organized as follows. Section 2 presents a review of common characteristics of DAOs and DAO categorization. Section 3 explains what DAO governance is and introduces different agenda-setting approaches. Section 4 reviews the existing voting schemes in DAOs. In Sec. 5, we examine dispute resolution options. Finally, Sec. 6 summarizes the essential insights of this paper and suggests areas for further research.

2. DAO Categorization

Different types of DAOs exist (Wang *et al.*, 2022). DAOs may run on distinct underlying blockchain platforms, are used in different areas of applications, and have their idiosyncratic rules of governance, amongst other features. This section discusses how DAOs can be categorized.

2.1. *Common characteristics of DAOs*

Despite the diversity, some common features can be observed in many DAOs as summarized in what follows (Wang *et al.*, 2019; Sims, 2021):

1. *Decentralization*. The objective of any DAO is to achieve operation, governance, and coordination among distributed network nodes or those who operate them, without the need for any central authority.
2. *Autonomy*. Ideally, smart contracts facilitate governance and coordination in a DAO. All nodes in a DAO network are hierarchically equal, and the decision-making power is distributed among members. Members can alter the rules through a voting process.
3. *Organized and ordered*. Conceptually, a DAO's management should be more orderly, as it relies on predefined rules written into smart contracts.[2]

2.2. *DAO categorization*

DAOs can be part of either of two categories. One is a native custom DAO. The first noteworthy DAO of this type was "The DAO", which was introduced by a group of programmers in April 2016 and deployed on the Ethereum Blockchain. Typically, experts with strong technical domain knowledge design and administer this form of DAO. Another example is MakerDAO (Sun *et al.*, 2022), which is focused on decentralized finance (DeFi). It was released in December 2017 (MakerDAO, 2020). Its community governs the Maker Protocol (one of the largest DApps on Ethereum). It uses cryptocurrency ETH as collateral to mint a stablecoin named DAI that can be used as a store of value on chain.

The second type of DAO leverages existing platforms. This category is also known as the DAO as-a-service. Platforms in this category provide infrastructure and allow members without domain blockchain knowledge to create a DAO using a customizable template.

---

[2] In a new empirical paper Feichtinger *et al.* (2023) find a high amount of pointless governance activity suggesting that the concept of a DAO is still nascent.

Examples for this type of DAO include Aragon,[3] DAOstack,[4] DAOhaus,[5] and Colony.[6] Another approach altogether, classifies DAOs based on their objectives. Table 1 provides a brief overview of eight different types.

Table 1. Types of DAO based on their objectives.

DAO Type	Description	Examples
Collector DAO	Pools funds from small investors to invest in projects as a community. Each contributor owns a share based on their contribution.	FlamingoDAO, ConstitutionDAO, PleasrDAO[a]
Grant DAO	Coordinates donation-based crowdfunding for nonprofit organizations.	Aave Grants DAO, MetaCartel, Compound Grants,[b] Uniswap Grants[c]
Media DAO	Organizes for community-driven media content where individual creators are entitled to a share of the profit.	BanklessDAO, Decrypt, GCR[d]
Protocol DAO	Governs decentralized protocols for DApps like borrowing and lending or decentralized exchanges.	MakerDAO, Uniswap, Yearn Finance, Aave,[e] Curve DAO[f]
Philanthropy DAO	Social responsibility DAOs support various objectives such as nutrition security, mental health, and climate change.	Big Green DAO
Venture (Investment) DAO	Blockchain-based venture capital that pools capital to invest in early-stage Web3 organizations.	Krause House DAO, MetaCartel Ventures, BitDAO,[g] The LAO[h]
Social DAO	Builds on social groups where like-minded individuals create and build the community. Entry barriers such as minimum token numbers may apply.	Friends with Benefits, SUSS DBAC DAO[i]
SubDAO	A DAO formulated by a subset of DAO members to facilitate specific functions such as operations, partnerships, marketing, treasury, and grants.	Balancer Protocol

[a] https://pleasr.org/.

[b] https://compound.finance/governance/proposals/40.

[c] https://www.unigrants.org/.

[d] https://globalcoinresearch.com/.

[e] https://aave.com/.

[f] https://curve.fi/#/ethereum/swap.

[g] https://www.bitdao.io/.

[h] https://www.thelao.io/.

[i] https://mirror.xyz/0x3Db51A64FF7812376005E8e617e42233e83118d2/-f5vkXvFPwFHPbhixixHCPQ4BybjATM6-AWv-yZTunM.

---

[3] https://blog.aragon.org/.

[4] https://alchemy.daostack.io/.

[5] https://daohaus.club/ 4https://colony.io/.

[6] https://colony.io.

3. DAO Governance

Analogous to the firm, for a DAO to succeed, grow and prosper, governance is paramount.

3.1. *What is DAO governance*

In the academic literature, we observe various definitions for DAO governance. In Williamson's (2005) study, governance in DAOs is described as "good order and effective arrangements", which was later revised in the context of blockchains to "the framework for accountability, roles, and decision-making power within an organization". In Introna's (2016) study, governance is defined as "a code of conduct for a group of independent actors, both human and nonhuman, who lack the power or authority to single-handedly make and implement decisions and policies". We define DAO governance as a class of rules defined in blockchain-based smart contracts, used to manage, and coordinate an organization's strategy and operations without a central authority. The members of a DAO are given voting rights to collectively decide on proposals. Such proposals ideally relate to important changes or decisions to be made. The role of the governance token is to confer such voting rights to members.

3.2. *Agenda setting*

In the context of the firm, the board of directors comes together to decide which proposals (important decision to be made) are eligible for voting by shareholders. Therefore, it sets the agenda. This small group of decision-makers, act as gatekeepers who are responsible for proposing and deciding what makes it onto the agenda. This approach has advantages and disadvantages. The advantage is that few actors can reach consensus fast and it is hard for individuals to abuse the system with many low-quality proposals (Sims, 2021). The disadvantage is that power is highly concentrated. Not all shareholders are allowed to propose matters to be added to the agenda for voting. It is questionable whether the board always acts in the best interest of shareholders.

On the other hand, in the DAO context, if all governance token holders are permitted to make a proposal that is immediately available for voting, this could also lead to various problems. For instance, if there is no effective barrier or filter to vet proposals before they are put forward to voters, there could be an excessive number of proposals put forward to voters who would simply be overwhelmed. In the decentralized world, it is already difficult to motivate voters to engage even if proposals are vetted in advance (Fritsch *et al.*, 2022), making this issue a significant matter. This challenge could be exacerbated if a malicious actor was to inundate the system with countless proposals, much like spam emails, as it may require minimal effort and cost to submit them. Another problem relates to token holders not having the necessary knowledge and/or expertise to vote on specific proposals. Separately, proposers might not have spent much effort investigating the issue and understanding possible consequences, before putting forward a proposal. This can decrease the quality of proposals put forward. A more hostile issue altogether relates to individual token holders intending to propose only with their interest in mind rather than what is best to achieve the common objectives of the DAO. Considering these issues, making proposals available for immediate voting can lead to a waste of limited resources (Feichtinger *et al.*, 2023).

Deciding on which proposals are put forward for voting is therefore critical for DAOs. We now review two types of agenda setting mechanisms that aim to address the issues described above, in a decentralized manner. To prevent members from submitting an excessive number of proposals, DAOs can impose a cost for proposal submission. A submitter will be charged a fee in tokens for every new proposal. For instance, Dash DAO charges five tokens (USD 70.18 per token as of February 26, 2023). Some DAOs also ask proposers to stake tokens for the duration of the proposal. Uniswap requires 10 million votes to submit an onchain proposal.[7] Fees and staking requirements will serve as a barrier to prevent frivolous and harmful proposals. Still, there is an ongoing debate on high fees and staking requirements. Do they create a hurdle for those who genuinely wish to propose important changes but unfortunately do not own enough tokens? This problem can partially be mitigated by refunding the fee if the proposal is voted for. The proposer can suggest the amount of refund in their proposal. The limitation here is the small token holders need to have sufficient tokens to enter the game. Also, the proposal fee does not necessarily have to be uniform among all participants. It can vary depending on the nature and value of a proposal (Wood, 2016). Another way to address the issue of excessive proposal submissions is to limit access based on reputation. Reputation can be gained by contributing to the DAO ecosystem in various ways. For example, in DAOstack, a member can gain reputation if they vote in line with the majority. They lose reputation if they vote against the majority. Those who put forward a winning proposal can also gain a reputation. In certain DAOs like Colony, participation recency also affects the reputation. That is, the reputation can decline over time if the member is not participating in the voting process continuously. Unlike tokens, reputation is not transferable.

[7] https://gov.uniswap.org/t/community-governance-process/7732.

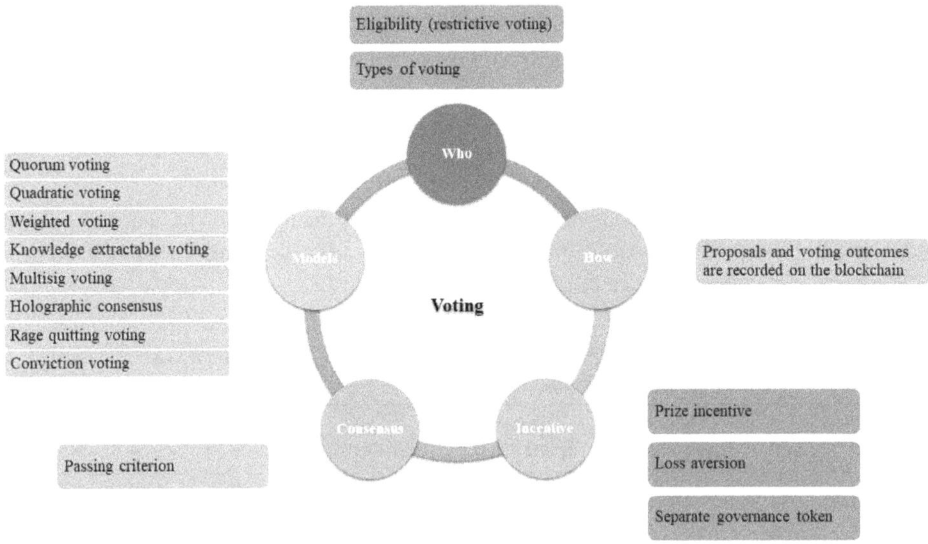

Fig. 2. Framework of DAO voting scheme.

Therefore, there is no benefit to split the reputation across multiple accounts. It is optimal develop reputation of a single account to become more powerful. Concentrated reputation in a single wallet avoids members from submitting a flood of proposals using several accounts.

4. Voting

Based on insights gained during our survey of the literature, we learned that a framework to assess voting schemes for DAO governance should include the aspects depicted at a high level in Fig. 2.

We now describe the framework in more detail.

4.1. *(Who) Who is entitled to vote*

In voting eligibility, there are three types of criteria: one-token one-vote, one-person one-vote, and restricted voting, as summarized in Table 2.

Although limiting the community of eligible voters may seem to contradict the principles of decentralization, restrictive voting systems are implemented to improve the decision-making process. Restricted voting identity types are shown in Table 3.

Table 2. Eligibility criteria.

Eligibility Criteria	Description
One-token one-vote	Each token held by a DAO member in one wallet represents one vote. Here, voting power may be centralized with few large holders commanding most votes.
One-person one-vote	Voting is limited to one vote per wallet. Due to the openness and anonymity of current blockchain systems token holders can create multiple wallets, thereby circumventing this criterium.
Restricted voting	Voting is restricted to specific members, for example, those with a minimum number of governance tokens or reputation holders. This may exclude small token holders from participating.

Table 3. Restricted voting identity types.

Restricted Voting	Definition	Examples
Members	The voting right is restricted to members who meet specific eligibility criteria, such as holding a minimum number of tokens or staking a certain amount of cryptocurrency in the DApp.	Dash DAO requires a minimum of 1,000 tokens to attain voting rights.
Reputation Holders	The voting right is restricted to members who possess a certain level of reputation. Reputation is a measure of a member's contribution to the DAO community and is typically earned by participating in governance or contributing to the project.	Aragon uses a reputation-based voting system where reputation is earned by participating in governance reputation is nontransferable.
Governance Token Holders	The voting right is restricted to holders of a specific governance token, which in some cases is separate from the DAO's main token.	MakerDAO runs the stable-coin DAI and has a separate governance token called MKR. Only MKR holders are entitled to vote on governance proposals.
Delegates	As a subset of the type of Governance Token Holders, we briefly describe as a mechanism that allows token holders to delegate their voting power to another member, who then participates in the decision-making process on their behalf. Delegation-based voting allows for more efficient and effective decision-making, as it enables token holders who may not have the time or expertise to participate actively in governance to participate and influence the future protocol's direction still passively.	In Uniswap,[a] token holders can delegate their voting power to a trusted, more experienced member who will ideally vote in the best interest of the DAO.

[a]https://docs.compound.finance/v2/governance/.

4.2. *(How) The voting process*

A DAO's voting process is comparable to a stockholders' meeting, where all eligible voters come together to vote on a proposal at hand. In a DAO, each voter will have one chance to vote. The vote cannot be reversed once immutably recorded on the blockchain. An advantageous characteristic of blockchain-based DAOs is that a proposal and its voting outcome can be inspected by others on the spot. However, a disadvantage is that not all eligible voters may participate in the process, leading to low turnout rates. Some DAOs have implemented a quorum to counter this issue of low turnout.

4.3. *Incentive mechanisms*

As discussed above, for decisions to be considered legitimate, a large enough voter turnout is necessary. Some DAOs have recorded voting participation as low as 3% or in some cases even lower. In addition to defining a quorum or using new ways of voting, incentive mechanisms to encourage participation could be significant to the success of DAO governance. There are several types of incentive mechanisms.

(a) Prize incentives
Voters get paid a prize to vote. Depending on the characteristics of the incentive payment to the voters, there are several possible implementations.

- *Wealth-based prize.* The prize size is based on the number of votes. Those who participate with more votes will receive a higher prize. Under the one-token one-vote scheme, those with more tokens will be rewarded with a larger incentive. Those with few tokens may receive a very small prize which may even discourage them from voting at all as they feel participation is not worth their while.
- *Lucky draw.* To overcome the drawback of the first implementation and to create a fairer chance for all voters, a random lucky draw can be used to decide on who will receive a prize. In this implementation, each voter stands an equal chance of winning the prize, regardless of token wealth. Sadly, lucky draws may attract voters who are not truly interested in the voting outcomes but participate to receive the prize only. Another problem with this approach is that members can also try to create multiple accounts to increase their odds of winning.
- *Deposit-based reward.* This is an implementation proposed by the team that launched the Dfinity blockchain. Those who wish to vote need to deposit

tokens into an account and they are not allowed to withdraw their tokens from this account for at least three months from the date of requesting release. The token holders are rewarded according to the number of tokens they deposited and on the number of proposals they voted on.

- *Reputation award.* Here, the incentive is not limited to tokens only, the DAO can also issue reputation credits to voters. Those who actively participate in the voting process will have higher reputation which in return can link to higher voting power.

(b) Loss aversion

Sometimes, members may not be motivated as the incentives provided may be (too) small. However, DAO members, like all other humans, display loss aversion. That is, no one likes losing their wealth. A loss aversion model (Bateman *et al.*, 2005) can be specified so that token holders could lose tokens if they fail to participate in the voting process.

(c) A separate (governance) token

In many ecosystems, the utility and governance features required for a functioning token economy are combined in a single token. But this does not have to be the case. Voters can use and be rewarded with a separate governance token which determines their voting power. For example, in the case of MakerDAO (Sun *et al.*, 2022), which provides a utility token, a stable-coin called DAI to its users, a separate token called MKR is used for governance. Holders of DAI have no say in the governance of the protocol and only MKR holders can vote. A member is allowed to hold both DAI and MKR at the same time. This type of design allows for separation of utility and governance rights.

4.4. *(Consensus) The consensus mechanism*

To reach a consensus on a voting outcome, a DAO needs to consider two features. The first is the passing criterion of a proposal. What voting result is considered a pass of the proposal? Based on the literature analyzed in this paper, there are a few commonly used criteria. The most straightforward criterion is by simple majority. Essentially, voters will vote "yes", "no", or "abstain" for a given proposal. Whichever category reaches the highest percentage of votes will determine the voting outcome. Additionally, to a simple majority, a super majority can be implemented. A super majority requires a minimum percentage of "yes" votes for any given proposal to pass. For example, Dash DAO requires at least 10% of the master nodes to vote "yes" for a proposal to pass. The second feature is based on minimum turnout and called quorum voting. Quorum voting requires voting participation to be no less than a certain threshold (e.g., 50% or 60%). If the quorum is not reached, the proposal will automatically be rejected.

4.5. *Voting models*

In the world of DAOs, currently, there are eight different voting schemes prevailing: Token-based Quorum Voting, Quadratic Voting, Weighted Voting (or Reputation-based Voting), Knowledge-Extractable Voting, Multisig Voting, Holographic Consensus, and Rage Quitting Voting and Conviction Voting.

The voting rules vary substantially. In Token-based Quorum Voting, voters utilize their tokens to cast their votes, and the voting process is considered valid only if a minimum quorum is met. Under Quadratic Voting, voters allocate their votes across multiple options, and they can express their preferences by allocating more voting power to a specific vote. Weighted Voting allows voters to have varying levels of influence based on factors such as reputation, contribution to the organization, or the number of tokens owned. In Knowledge-Extractable Voting, voters are required to solve a computational puzzle or answer a question to demonstrate their expertise thus the model can prevent Sybil attacks in which one member would create multiple fake identities to manipulate the voting outcome. Multisig Voting requires multiple parties to sign off on a proposal for it to be deemed valid. Holographic Consensus involves voters utilizing a scale to indicate their level of agreement with a proposal, which is then displayed as a hologram. Rage Quitting Voting enables voters to withdraw their funds from the organization if they disagree with the result of a vote. Under Conviction Voting, voters assign tokens to proposals, and these tokens are locked up until the proposal obtains a specific level of support (Ding *et al.*, 2023). Each voting scheme has its own advantages and disadvantages. To cater to the specific needs or scenarios of a platform, hybrid schemes can be utilized.

5. Dispute Resolution

5.1. *The necessity of dispute resolution*

Theoretically, atomic settlement of smart contracts powering DAOs should reduce dispute risk. But we must admit that dispute risk cannot disappear completely. Disputes within DAOs may occur in particular in the following situations (Sims, 2021; Guillaume and Riva, 2022; Aouidef *et al.*, 2021):

- Flawed code in smart contracts causes economic harm to all or individual members of the DAO. This risk is now known as "smart contract risk" (Harvey *et al.*, 2021). Example: The DAO hack[8] in 2016.
- The smart contracts cannot accommodate future requirements of the DAO. This is of particular significance in emergency situations where the risk of disputes among DAO members will inevitably arise. Example: Harvest Finance dispute in 2020.[9]
- Issues related to meta governance. If a proposal violates the constitution of DAO, its members have the right to dispute resolution. Here, a mechanism is used decide whether to overturn the proposal. Example: MakerDAO faced a dispute when a proposal was submitted to change the liquidation mechanism for collateralized dept positions on the platform in 2020.[10]
- Disputes relating to data quality provided by oracles. Oracles are third-party services providing external information to a blockchain network. They are often considered a single point of failure since it is hard to implement them in a completely trustless manner. Example: A dispute on the Augur platform raised questions about the reliability of oracles used to operate the prediction market in 2019.[11]
- Ambiguities can be introduced when converting a legal contract into a smart contract. Example: The DAO hack in 2016 highlighted the need for clear and accurate legal language in smart contracts.

Considering these issues, it is essential to study what options for dispute resolution can (and cannot) be used in the context of DAOs.

5.2. *Critical factors and methods for DAO dispute resolution*

First, we list critical factors for effective DAO dispute resolution from the literature (Sims, 2021; Guillaume and Riva, 2022; Aouidef *et al.*, 2021):

- When choosing a dispute resolution mechanism, we need to consider the cost and whether it makes sense to be applied to high-value and low-value claims.
- How long will it take from raising a dispute to resolving it? A good dispute resolution method should be time-efficient.

---

[8] https://www.coindesk.com/learn/2016/06/25/understanding-the-dao-attack/.

[9] https://www.coindesk.com/tech/2020/10/26/harvest-finance-24m-attack-triggers-570m-bank-run-in-latest-defi-exploit/.

[10] https://insights.glassnode.com/what-really-happened-to-makerdao/.

[11] https://blog.coinfund.io/trolling-with-rep-c5b6e1e0461.

- DAO members often come from different jurisdictions. Therefore, it is necessary that the method can be effective across jurisdictions.
- Disputes within DAOs may require specific subject matter expertise, in particular coding of smart contracts and legal expertise. Without this combined knowledge it may be difficult to resolve disputes (Allen and Hunn, 2022).
- DAO members are often anonymous. Even if a dispute resolution mechanism is theoretically sound, it may still be difficult to enforce if it relies on knowing the identity of parties.

Next, we examine various dispute resolution methods considering the above issues (Sims, 2021). We find that they generally do not meet DAO requirements:

- Courts: Courts (Gill *et al.*, 2015) are the traditional dispute resolution institutions that individuals use. Although there are well-trained judges, they may not be able to rule correctly as they may lack the understanding of dynamics and technology related to DAOs or smart contracts. Even if the judge makes a just judgement, it is difficult to enforce the decision as DAO members are usually anonymous. In addition, the time required to reach a resolution and associated costs is high.
- Tribunals: Tribunals (Elliott and Thomas, 2012; Salter, 2017) are cheaper and faster than courts. And they can also be used for low-value claims. But they also do not work well with disputes if the individuals involved come from several different jurisdictions.
- Industry Schemes: Some companies construct their own dispute resolution mechanisms for resolving disputes between the company's clients and their members. Their advantage is that the fees will be lower than courts and tribunals. They also will use experts in this field to resolve disputes. However, most industry schemes (Authority, 2017; Noone and Ojelabi, 2020) are, again, jurisdiction-specific. Considering that the individuals involved in DAO disputes often come from different jurisdictions, industry schemes are not well suited to resolve DAO's disputes.
- Mediation: Mediation (Goldberg *et al.*, 2020) uses neutral third parties to help resolve disputes. Mediation costs are relatively high, so it is more suitable for sufficiently high-value claims. In addition, the final decision does not have a strong binding force on the individuals involved in the dispute.
- Arbitration: The arbitrator (Goldberg *et al.*, 2020) hears the dispute and provides an award. Unlike mediation, an arbitration award is binding on the parties and can be enforced by courts in different jurisdictions. However, it only works for high-value claims, and parties need to be known.

Table 4. A comparison of various dispute resolution methods.

Dispute Resolution Method	Cost	Efficiency	International Applicability	DAO Professional Knowledge	Anonymous Member Compatibility	DAO Readiness
Courts	High	Low	No	Limited	No	No
Tribunals	Low	High	No	Limited	No	No
Industry Schemes	Low	High	No	Limited	No	No
Mediation	High	High	Yes	Limited	No	No
Arbitration	High	Low	Yes	Limited	No	No
ODR	Low	High	Yes	Limited	No	No

- Online Dispute Resolution (ODR): ODR (Deffains *et al.*, 2005; Mania, 2015) is a faster and cheaper method compared to the methods outlined above. Both eBay and Alibaba have created their own ODR mechanisms to resolve disputes. They use algorithms to ensure fairness and efficiency in decision-making. However, their dispute mechanism can only be used to resolve disputes related to their companies, not DAO disputes.

Table 4 presents a comparison of various dispute resolution methods.

5.3. *Decentralized dispute resolution services*

To address the issue of DAO readiness, researchers have recently proposed Decentralized Dispute Resolution Services (DDRS) (Metzger, 2018; Ast and Deffains, 2020; Aouidef *et al.*, 2021; Perdrisat, 2021; Saygili *et al.*, 2022; Lee and Cui, 2022). DDRS are similar to a "digital court" that uses blockchain technology, crowdsources jurors and leverages economic incentives to provide fair rulings (Aouidef *et al.*, 2021).

Figure 3 depicts the general process of DDRS.

Once a dispute arises within a DAO, a small group of jurors is selected randomly from a pool of token holders who have staked their tokens as collateral. These jurors are responsible for deciding the outcome of the dispute. If one or both parties involved in the dispute disagree with the outcome, they can appeal at a higher court. Appealing is costly. Jurors who vote in line with the majority decision receive a reward, while those who vote against it are penalized, their staked tokens get slashed. DDRS employ the Schelling Point mechanism, which operates

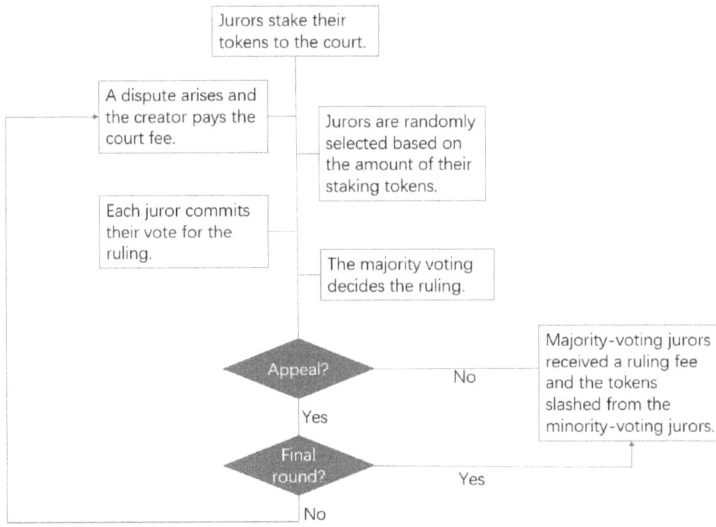

Fig. 3. Flowchart of DDRS.

on the principle that if people anticipate others to vote honestly, they will have the incentive to do so to align with the majority. This mutual expectation of honesty among participants makes it possible to rely on others to vote truthfully (Aouidef *et al.*, 2021). DDRS are a new generation of ODR based on blockchain, using smart contracts to enforce the results of dispute resolution. DDRS can operate without knowing the identity of the involved parties. All they need are the public keys of the involved parties. Today's DDRS' can be divided into two categories: single layer and multi-layer, as shown in Table 5.

6. Conclusion

In this paper, we conduct a systematic review of research articles investigating DAOs and DAO governance, to complement the existing, but nascent literature. We highlight common DAO characteristics such as decentralization, autonomy and being (more) organized and orderly. We categorize DAOs (native, DAO as-a-service, or by objective) and share examples of real-world DAO applications, for example, MakerDAO, a DeFi platform. We zoom in on DAO governance and discuss agenda setting and voting. We find that free submission of proposals leads to spam-like submissions. Charging a fee or requiring staking for the duration of the proposal can reduce proposal-spam. Incentive design is critical for DAO governance. Defining voting eligibility criteria, prize incentives, loss aversion and

Table 5. Existing DDRS types.

Category	DDRS Mechanism	Description
Single Layer	Kleros[a]	Uses crowdsourcing to resolve disputes with jurors who have relevant professional knowledge. Jurors stake tokens and are paid only when they vote in line with the majority. Appeals are allowed but costs raise sharply.
	Aragon Court[b]	Also uses crowdsourcing similar to Kleros but allows members of DAOs to submit disputes before proposals are voted on.
Multi-layer	Jur[c]	Provides three different layers to resolve disputes based on the value of the dispute. The Court Layer is the first layer for highest value disputes, the Open Layer is for small-value disputes, and the Community Layer is for medium-value disputes.
	Juris[d]	Offers three different layers to resolve disputes and requires parties to include Juris' arbitration code in their smart contract. Once a dispute arises, the Juris Protocol can freeze the smart contract.

Notes: Currently, most of the above DDRS methods can only be applied to binary cases, those that only have two possible outcomes in a dispute. For example, you can either approve the proposal or reject it. Real disputes are usually more complex and cannot be represented by binary cases. This is a significant limitation of DDRS.

[a] https://kleros.io/.

[b] https://github.com/aragon/aragon-court.

[c] https://jur.io/.

[d] https://juris-marketing.netlify.app/.

having a separate governance token may facilitate a sound voting process. Separately we discuss when dispute resolution mechanisms are required and find that traditional mechanisms are not suitable in the context of DAOs and that decentralized single or multi-layer dispute resolution mechanisms are promising developments. We anticipate that our work can provide useful insights and references for researchers or industrial practitioners who wish to delve deeper into this area. Many opportunities for future research exist. Where delegation exists, what is the role of it in the context of DAO governance, and what are its effects on token prices? What motivates delegators to delegate their voting power to other individuals/members in the first place? And when do they un-delegate and why? What other approaches exist to address low participation in governance be overcome? Which methods can legitimate DAO members use to counter what Feichtinger *et al.* (2023) call "pointless governance activity"? What approaches can DAO members design to promote more decentralization of token holdings across wallets? And how can legal responsibilities and onchain DAO governance be harmonized? These are only a few questions that will help researchers can investigate.

Insights identified will benefit practitioners to better understand DAOs and their dynamics in the future.

References

Allen, J., and P. Hunn (editors), 2022, *Smart Legal Contracts: Computable Law in Theory and Practice*, Oxford University Press, Oxford.

Aouidef, Y., F. Ast, and B. Deffains, 2021, Decentralized Justice: A Comparative Analysis of Blockchain Online Dispute Resolution Projects, *Frontiers in Blockchain* 4, 3.

Ast, F., and B. Deffains, 2020, When Online Dispute Resolution Meets Blockchain: The Birth of Decentralized Justice, *Stanford Journal of Blockchain Law & Policy* 4, 1.

Atzori, M., 2015, Blockchain Technology and Decentralized Governance: Is the State Still Necessary? SSRN 2709713.

Authority, K. R., 2017, Alternative Dispute Resolution, Presentation to ICPAK IPSAS Workshop.

Bateman, I., D. Kahneman, A. Munro, C. Starmer, and R. Sugden, 2005, Testing Competing Models of Loss Aversion: An Adversarial Collaboration, *Journal of Public Economics* 89(8), 1561–1580.

De Filippi, P., and S. Hassan, 2018, Blockchain Technology as a Regulatory Technology: From Code is Law to Law is Code, arXiv:1801.02507.

De Filippi, P., and S. Hassan, 2021, Decentralized Autonomous Organization, *Internet Policy Review* 10(2), 1–10, https://doi.org/10.14763/2021.2.1556.

Deffains, B. *et al.*, 2005, Efficiency of Online Dispute Resolution: A Case Study, *Communications and Strategies* 60, 201.

Ding, Q. X., D. K. C. Lee, W. B. Xu, Z. G. Wang, and ChatGPT, 2023, Voting Schemes in DAO Governance, Working Paper.

El Faqir, Y., J. Arroyo, and S. Hassan, 2020, An Overview of Decentralized Autonomous Organizations on the Blockchain, in *Proceedings of the 16th International Symposium on Open Collaboration*, Association for Computing Machinery, New York, pp. 1–8.

Elliott, M., and R. Thomas, 2012, Tribunal Justice and Proportionate Dispute Resolution, *The Cambridge Law Journal* 71(2), 297–324.

Feichtinger, R., R. Fritsch, Y. Vonlanthen, and R. Wattenhofer, 2023, The Hidden Shortcomings of (D)AOs — An Empirical Study of On-Chain Governance, arXiv: 2302.12125.

Fritsch, R., M. Muller, and R. Wattenhofer, 2022, Analyzing Voting Power in Decentralized Governance: Who Controls DAOs?, arXiv:2204.01176.

Gill, J., R. Carroll, C. To, M. Unger, A. Mourre, C. Oetiker, J. Essebier, and A. Hironaka, 2015, Dispute Resolution International. *The Journal of Dispute Resolution Section of the International Bar Association* 9(2), 91–184.

Goldberg, S. B., F. E. Sander, N. H. Rogers, and S. R. Cole, 2020, *Dispute Resolution: Negotiation, Mediation, Arbitration, and Other Processes*, Aspen Publishing.

Guillaume, F., and S. Riva, 2022, Blockchain Dispute Resolution for Decentralized Autonomous Organizations: The Rise of Decentralized Autonomous Justice, in *Blockchain and Private International Law*, Brill Nijhoff.

Guo, Y., Z. Wan, and X. Cheng, 2022, When Blockchain Meets Smart Grids: A Comprehensive Survey, *High-Confidence Computing* 2, 100059.

Harvey, C. R., A. Ramachandran, and J. Santoro, 2021, *DeFi and the Future of Finance*, John Wiley & Sons.

Hassan, S. and P. De Filippi, 2021, Decentralized Autonomous Organization, *Internet Policy Review* 10(2), 1–10.

Hsieh, Y. Y., J. P. Vergne, P. Anderson, K. Lakhani, and M. Reitzig, 2018, Bitcoin and the Rise of Decentralized Autonomous Organizations, *Journal of Organization Design* 7(1), 1–16.

Introna, L. D., 2016, Algorithms, Governance, and Governmentality: On Governing Academic Writing, *Science, Technology, & Human Values* 41(1), 17–49.

Keele, S. *et al.*, 2007, Guidelines for Performing Systematic Literature Reviews in Software Engineering, EBSE Technical Report.

Lee, D. K. C. (editor), 2020, *Artificial Intelligence, Data and Blockchain in a Digital Economy*, Vol. 3, World Scientific.

Lee, D. K. C., D. Ding, and C. Guan (editors), 2021, *Financial Management in the Digital Economy*, Vol. 6, World Scientific.

Lee, D. K. C., J. Lim, K. F. Phoon, and Y. Wang, (editors), 2022, *Applications and Trends in Fintech I: Governance, AI, and Blockchain Design Thinking*, Vol. 4, World Scientific.

Lee, W. K., and Y. Cui, 2022, Should gig platforms decentralize dispute resolution? SSRN 3719630.

Liu, Y., Q. Lu, L. Zhu, H.-Y. Paik, and M. Staples, 2021, A Systematic Literature Review on Blockchain Governance, arXiv:2105.05460.

Lo, S. W., Y. Wang, and D. K. C. Lee, 2021, *Blockchain and Smart Contracts: Design Thinking and Programming for Fintech*, Vol. 4, World Scientific.

MakerDAO, 2020, White Paper, https://makerdao.com/en/whitepaper/.

Mania, K., 2015, Online Dispute Resolution: The Future of Justice, *International Comparative Jurisprudence* 1(1), 76–86.

Metzger, J., 2018, Decentralized Justice in the Era of Blockchain, *International Journal of Online Dispute Resolution* 5, 69.

Noone, M. A., and L. A. Ojelabi, 2020, Alternative Dispute Resolution and Access to Justice in Australia, *International Journal of Law in Context* 16(2), 108–127.

Perdrisat, S., 2021, Case Study of Sociotechnical Imaginaries in the Making: Kleros Decentralized Dispute Resolution Protocol, Master of Arts Thesis, Tallinn University of Technology.

Rozas, D., A. Tenorio-Fornes, S. Díaz-Molina, and S. Hassan, 2021, When Ostrom Meets Blockchain: Exploring the Potentials of Blockchain for Commons Governance, *SAGE Open* 11(1), 21582440211002526.

Salter, S., 2017, Online Dispute Resolution and Justice System Integration: British Columbia's Civil Resolution Tribunal, *Windsor Yearbook of Access to Justice/Recueil Annuel de Windsor d'Accès à la Justice* 34(1), 112–129.

Saygili, M., I. E. Mert, and O. B. Tokdemir, 2022, A Decentralized Structure to Reduce and Resolve Construction Disputes in a Hybrid Blockchain Network, *Automation in Construction* 134, 104056.

Sims, A., 2021, Decentralised Autonomous Organisations: Governance, Dispute Resolution and Regulation, Dispute Resolution and Regulation (May 31, 2021). Available at SSRN: https://ssrn.com/abstract=3971228.

Singh, M., and S. Kim, 2019, Blockchain Technology for Decentralized Autonomous Organizations, *Advances in Computers* 115, 115–140.

Sun, X., C. Stasinakis, and G. Sermpinis, 2022, Decentralization Illusion in DeFi: Evidence from MakerDAO, arXiv:2203.16612.

Sun, X., X. Chen, C. Stasinakis, and G. Sermpinis, 2022, Multiparty Democracy in Decentralized Autonomous Organization (DAO): Evidence from MakerDAO, arXiv:2210.11203.

Wang, Q., G. Yu, Y. Sai, C. Sun, L. D. Nguyen, S. Xu, and S. Chen, 2022, An Empirical Study on Snapshot DAOs, arXiv:2211.15993.

Wang, S., W. Ding, J. Li, Y. Yuan, L. Ouyang, and F.-Y. Wang, 2019, Decentralized Autonomous Organizations: Concept, Model, and Applications, *IEEE Transactions on Computational Social Systems* 6(5), 870–878.

Williamson, O. E., 2005, The Economics of Governance, *American Economic Review* 95(2), 1–18.

Wood, G., 2016, Polkadot: Vision for a Heterogeneous Multi-chain Framework, *White Paper* 21(2327), 4662.

Wright, A., and P. De Filippi, 2015, Decentralized Blockchain Technology and the Rise of Lex Cryptographia, SSRN 2580664.

A Commentary on "Building a Sustainable Future: Exploring Green Finance, Regenerative Finance, and Green Financial Technology"

Xin (Cindy) Deng and Denise Lai

*Nanyang Business School,
Nanyang Technological University, Singapore*

There is no denying that climate change is a serious and urgent problem that everyone has a stake in. The UN report on climate change warns that the time to limit global warming to 1.5 degrees Celsius is "now or never," as the IPCC report written by leading scientists laid bare the fact that there was a "yawning gap between climate pledges and reality." In the age of digital transformation, the finance industry has the technological tools to contribute to sustainable goals by helping firms transform into greener businesses with more sustainable operations. "Building a Sustainable Future: Exploring Green Finance, Regenerative Finance, and Green Financial Technology" discusses how green financial technology ("green fintech") leverages technology to support sustainable finance; it also reviews the latest advancements in green technologies and how they are utilized to mitigate the effects of climate change.

Digital technologies, as enablers of improved efficiency and cost minimization, are engines of innovation and growth, allowing firms to reimagine their businesses and gain competitive advantage in new markets. Reaching every facet of business operation, the ways in which we collect, store, share, and analyze data have been reshaped by technology, which provides the basis for resolving sustainability constraints.

First, the quality of sustainable data is considered the biggest barrier to the adoption of sustainable finance according to a survey by BlackRock.[1] Various digital technologies help financial institutions not only capture large volumes of data at faster speeds and lower costs but also increase the quality of the data obtained. For example, the Internet of Things (IoT) enables physical objects equipped with sensors and computing power to be connected and to exchange data via the Internet. The collection and reporting of ESG metrics, such as carbon footprint, water usage, and energy efficiency, can be more streamlined. Developments in satellite technology and natural language processing (NLP) have also allowed data to be collected from satellite images and millions of unstructured data sources. With such alternative data sources, stakeholders need not rely solely on firms' disclosure and are able to monitor corporate ESG performance and measure firms' exposure to environmental risk on a more timely basis. Verification of firms' disclosure using alternative data from various sources also helps stakeholders hold firms accountable. Thus, technology has increased transparency and ensured market integrity by allowing high-quality data to be collected and assessed by stakeholders for scrutinization.

Second, after data have been collected, their storage and sharing become the next critical step. As sustainability issues cannot be tackled by any single country, corporation, or organization on its own, sharing of information allows effective coordination of stakeholders in order to maximize every dollar invested in the pursuit of ESG goals. Hence, secure data storage and efficient information sharing are critical as individuals, businesses, and governments come together to tackle sustainability issues. Blockchain technology has made this more efficient using distributed ledgers that hold and structure information in an irreversible timeline of data when implemented in a decentralized nature. This ensures that data are

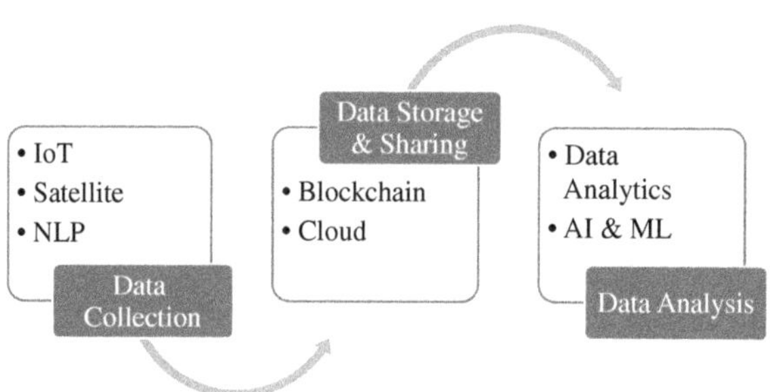

Figure 1. Technologies as Enablers of Data Collection, Storage and Sharing, and Data Analysis

[1] https://ir.blackrock.com/news-and-events/press-releases/press-releases-details/2020/BlackRock-Survey-Shows-Acceleration-of-Sustainable-Investing/default.aspx.

stored securely and easily retrieved when needed. Cloud technology has also improved the efficiency of data storage, its virtually unlimited storage capacity allowing firms to scale up quickly at lower costs. Both blockchain and cloud technology have increased the ease and security of data storage. Beyond that, these technologies also facilitate the sharing of information.

Finally, the proliferation of data analytics and artificial intelligence (AI) has increased the capacity of financial institutions to generate insights from large volumes of data. Using data analytics tools and AI, this process can be sped up so that investors can make better economic decisions quickly, thus helping firms gain access to more capital for their ESG projects. For regulatory bodies, data analytics also facilitates decision-making processes such that they can make swift adjustments to policies and regulations to promote financing for sustainability-related activities and prevent activities of greenwashing.

The integration of blockchain, IoT, advanced data analytics, distributed ledger technology, ML, and AI has empowered businesses in their pursuit of ESG goals by increasing the transparency, accuracy, and efficiency of their operations. Yet, there are still many challenges when it comes to the effective utilization of these technologies and the implementation of fintech-based solutions. One key challenge for many firms in the adoption of these technologies is having a robust understanding of them. As many of these technologies are still nascent, their complexity could hamper public understanding of how these technologies function. More critically, the modernity of these technologies also means that there is a lack of standardization of procedures and protocols for the integration of certain products such as microgrids in their respective markets. Without such standardization, interoperability across different business ecosystems may be challenging because the product integration process would need to be repeated when used in different markets. Relatedly, the lack of a strong and well-defined regulatory regime hinders the adoption of technology in relation to addressing ESG issues.

Building a Sustainable Future: Exploring Green Finance, Regenerative Finance, and Green Financial Technology*

Chia Mei Shih†

Node for Inclusive Fintech (NiFT), Singapore University of Social Sciences Singapore 599494, Singapore
carmenshihcm@suss.edu.sg

Andrzej Gwizdalski

University of Western Australia, Perth, WA 6009, Australia

Xin Deng

Nanyang Business School, Nanyang Technological University Singapore 639798, Singapore

This paper presents an overview of sustainable finance and focuses on the crucial role of green and regenerative finance in promoting sustainability in the contemporary world. It discusses how green financial technology (green fintech) leverages technology to support sustainable finance and reviews the latest advancements in green technologies, and how they are utilized to mitigate the effects of climate change. In addition, it highlights the importance of governance in these two areas of sustainable finance. Several real-life case stories are also presented to illustrate the successful applications of green technologies by organizations and individuals to mitigate the effects of climate change and achieve sustainability goals. In sum, the overarching goal of this paper is to demonstrate how harnessing the power of green and regenerative finance and green fintech is crucial in ensuring a sustainable future for all.

*This Chapter was originally published in the *World Scientific Annual Review of Fintech*, Vol. 1, No. 1, doi: 10.1142/S2811004823500021.

†Corresponding author.

Keywords: Climate change; sustainability; sustainable finance; green finance; regenerative finance; green financial technologies; fintech.

The future of capital is green.

Mr. Ravi Menon, Managing Director of the Monetary Authority of Singapore

1. Introduction

The alarming increase in greenhouse gas emissions and environmental degradation resulting from human activities has caused a rapid decline in biodiversity, with serious consequences for economic growth, societal stability, and the quality of life. To prevent a potential ecological catastrophe, it is crucial that immediate action be taken to address these pressing environmental concerns and ensure a sustainable future for all. That is, a systemic shift towards a sustainable economy is warranted to address the global ecological emergency.[1] While there is no single solution to this complex challenge, a collective global effort is necessary to achieve environmental sustainability. Consequently, global frameworks, and agreements, such as the Sustainable Development Goals, the UN Framework Convention on Climate Change, and the Paris Agreement, have been set up to guide the process.

One of the key goals of the Paris Agreement is to limit global temperature rise to 1.5°C above pre-industrial levels (Assembly, 2015; UNFCCC, n.d.). The threshold is set at this level because it is widely acknowledged that any increase beyond this would lead to severe and potentially devasting consequences for the environment, society and the economy.[2] In fact, the Intergovernmental Panel on Climate Change (IPCC 2018, UNEP 2020) suggests that, to meet this 1.5°C target, all countries in the world need to achieve net-zero carbon dioxide (CO_2) emissions by 2050, a goal known as carbon neutrality.[3] This will require significant investment

[1]Environmental sustainability refers to the practice of using natural resources responsibly so that they are not depleted by use.

[2]The impacts of such a temperature rise could include more frequent and severe heatwaves, droughts, floods, storms, sea level rise, and the loss of biodiversity and ecosystems. These changes have serious implications for food security, human health, economic growth, and social stability, particularly for vulnerable populations in developing countries.

[3]To achieve carbon neutrality, the frameworks urge taking actions alongside three key dimensions: environmental, social, and economic. The environmental dimension of sustainability involves mitigating global warming by altering or avoiding human activities such as intensive agriculture, overexploitation of natural resources and over-consumption of energy and materials. The social dimension

in new technologies and infrastructure across all sectors of the economy, including energy, transportation, buildings, industry, and agriculture.[4]

Green finance and green financial technologies (or green fintech) have emerged as a response to address climate change within the economic dimension. Green finance helps to drive the progress towards a sustainable global economy by providing financial resources and investment opportunities for projects and initiatives that provide environmental benefits. The development of green finance instruments has been critical to the growth of green finance. These instruments include green bonds and loans, carbon finance instruments, and sustainable investment funds. To support the green finance ecosystem and accelerate the adoption of green finance, financial technologies (fintech) such as blockchain technology, artificial intelligence (AI), and Internet of Things (IoT), are increasingly being used to improve the efficiency, transparency, and security of green finance transactions.

The importance of green finance and green fintech cannot be overstated. As the world faces urgent environmental challenges, the financial sector has a critical role to play in supporting the transition to a sustainable and resilient global economy. Green finance and green fintech are at the forefront of this movement. The purpose of this paper is to explore the current state of green finance and green fintech, including trends, challenges, recent developments, and governance. By examining these areas, we hope to gain a deeper understanding of the risks and opportunities associated with green finance and green fintech, and the role they can play in supporting the transition to a sustainable future.

Within the field of sustainable finance, a new approach called regenerative finance (or ReFi) has emerged to support investments that promote ecological health, social well-being, and economic resilience. ReFi builds on the progress made in green finance and green fintech, and incorporates the latest innovations in

---

of sustainability recognizes the importance of ensuring that all members of society have access to basic human needs, such as food, water, healthcare, and education. This dimension recognizes that human well-being is interconnected with the well-being of the environment. Factors such as social equity, human rights, labor standards, community development, and social justice are critical aspects of this dimension. The economic dimension of sustainability recognizes the importance of creating economic systems that support long-term sustainable development. This dimension recognizes that economic development and environmental protection are not mutually exclusive but must be integrated to achieve sustainability. The main approaches of this dimension include promoting sustainable business practices, reducing waste, and adopting innovative green technologies that minimize the environmental impact of economic activities.

[4]For example, countries need to build new infrastructure and upgrade existing systems to transit to renewable sources of energy and invest in energy storage solutions to ensure a reliable and consistent supply of energy.

decentralized finance using blockchain technologies. At the same time, ReFi also draws from older, more holistic approaches to sustainable economic systems, such as Fullerton's Regenerative Capitalism (2015). Compared to green finance, which focuses on creating financial instruments that lessen the environmental burden and promote sustainable practices, ReFi takes the sustainability paradigm to the next level by not only mitigating environmental damage, but also regenerating the natural systems that have been impacted by human activities. In adopting a comprehensive view of the interconnectedness of social, economic, and ecological systems, with an adequately aligned choice of decentralized technologies, ReFi aims to create a financial system with a long-term perspective that emphasizes the regeneration of natural and social capital to build a sustainable future.

To increase the efficiency and effectiveness of ReFi strategies, green finance and green fintech can be used to support and complement these environmental efforts. Specifically, green finance and green fintech can provide the financial infrastructure and technology that are needed to develop and scale ReFi initiatives.[5] Combining ReFi with green finance and green fintech can create a powerful and comprehensive approach to sustainable finance. By leveraging the strengths of these areas, a more holistic approach can be created to support the transition to a more sustainable and regenerative economy.

The rest of this paper is organized as follows. Section 2 provides an overview of sustainable finance, which includes green finance and ReFi, and elaborates on how green fintech leverages on technology to support these two areas of finance. Section 3 describes the current state of the art in green technologies. Section 4 discusses the governance aspects of green finance and green fintech. Section 5 presents several real-life case studies of entities that are successfully using green technologies to mitigate the effects of climate change and achieve their sustainability goals. Section 6 concludes the paper.

2. Sustainable Finance and Beyond: Green Finance, ReFi, and the Emerging Role of Green Fintech

Climate change is one of the biggest environmental challenges facing the world today. As human activities such as the combustion of fossil fuels, deforestation and industrial processes cause long-term changes in temperature and weather patterns, the impacts of climate change continue to pose a significant threat to not only the

[5] For example, green bonds can be used to support regenerative agriculture and clean energy, while green fintech can provide innovative technologies to streamline and automate the financing of these projects.

environment and society, but also the global economy. Traditional finance has often been criticized for contributing to these problems by providing financing to companies engaged in activities that are environmentally harmful or socially irresponsible. Addressing the effects of climate change requires significant investment in sustainable initiatives. In fact, the global new investment made in renewable energy in just the first half of 2022 summed to as much as $226 billion (BloombergNEF, 2022). Therefore, there is a growing need for more sustainable forms of finance, leading to the development of green finance, which aims to fund investment projects that are both environmentally and socially responsible.

To address the slow growth of green finance, green fintech emerged to provide innovative solutions that make it easy for investors to finance environmentally sustainable projects.[6] Green fintech refers to the use of financial technology to increase the flow of capital to environmentally sustainable projects. For example, green fintech platforms can provide investors with real-time information about the environmental performance of the projects they are investing in, as well as digital tools to assess the environmental risks and impacts of investment opportunities. These data and tools can streamline the investment process, increase the efficiency of green financing, and reduce transaction costs. The coupling and coordination between green finance and economic growth can therefore be improved by creating new channels for investment and improving the flow of information from project developers to investors.

Green fintech can also leverage emerging financial technologies such as blockchain and digital currencies to create new ways of financing green projects. For example, blockchain-based financing platforms can allow investors to fund green projects directly, without the need for intermediaries such as banks or traditional financial institutions. This can potentially reduce the costs and administrative burden associated with traditional financing options and increase the availability of funding for high technical value green innovation. Finally, green fintech platforms can also help to increase transparency and accountability in the green financing process by providing investors with better information and greater visibility of the impact of their investments. This can help to build trust in the green financing ecosystem and encourage more investment in high technical value green innovation.

A strong advocate for the adoption of green fintech, Sopnendu Mohanty, the Chief Fintech Officer of the Monetary Authority of Singapore (MAS, n.d.) highlights the importance of sustainability in the financial industry. In an interview

[6] A multitude of studies have shed light on the various technologies and technological approaches available and their effectiveness in combating climate change (Bel and Joseph, 2018; Jiang *et al.*, 2017; Li and Wang, 2017; Wang *et al.*, 2021).

with Azil and Sengupta (2022), Mohanty discusses about the role of fintech in driving green finance and how Singapore is positioning itself as a hub for green fintech. He believes that green fintech has the potential to not only drive positive social and environmental impact, but also create new business opportunities. In his opinion, the financial sector plays a critical role in advancing sustainability goals in that fintech innovation can help to unlock new sources of capital for sustainability investments, while improving the transparency and accountability of financial transactions. By using fintech to promote green finance, investors can do well and do good i.e., earn financial returns while doing good for the environment and society. This approach can potentially drive the largest capital reallocation ever. For it to work, there is a need to educate investors about the benefits of green fintech and provide them with the necessary knowledge and technical skills to effectively apply fintech to achieve the green finance goals.

Besides deploying green fintech to promote green finance, emerging decentralized technologies can also be used to support a new field of sustainable finance, namely ReFi. Traditionally, sustainable finance has focused on mitigating the negative environmental impacts of economic activities and promoting green, sustainable economic growth. ReFi, on the other hand, goes beyond just economic sustainability and aims to restore natural ecosystems and improve social well-being through the use of financial tools and technologies such as open-source public and decentralized blockchain and Decentralized Autonomous Organizations (DAOs),[7] to support regenerative agriculture, conservation, and the restoration of natural resources.[8] In doing so, we can not only protect the environment and reduce the impact of climate change, but also promote social equity and economic resilience. In sum, ReFi represents a shift away from traditional financial practices that prioritize short-term profit and is a holistic approach that emphasizes long-term sustainability, social well-being, and environmental health.

3. Advancements in Green Technologies: A Review of the Current State of the Art

Green fintech is a rapidly growing field that is leveraging various technologies to support and promote sustainable financial practices. Some of the key technologies used in green fintech include blockchain, AI, IoT, big data analytics, and

---

[7] See Diaz-Valdivia and Poblet (2022).

[8] For example, blockchain technology can be used to create a secure and transparent record of sustainable practices in agriculture, while AI can help identify areas that are at high risk of environmental degradation and prioritize conservation efforts.

crowdfunding platforms. With these technologies, green fintech is making it easy for individuals, businesses, and governments to invest in green projects, thereby ultimately contributing to a more sustainable future.

3.1. *Blockchain*

A blockchain is a distributed digital ledger that securely records and shares information across a decentralized network of participating computers, without the need for a centralized overseeing party.[9] Each block is essentially a database that records digital transactions in a transparent and tamper-proof manner, linked with the previous block in the chain using cryptography, which generates a unique code, or hash, for each block. The growing interest in blockchain technology has spurred extensive research and developments in this field. As a result, it is highly likely that many of the challenges associated with the technology will soon be addressed, allowing for blockchains to be utilized in their most valued capacities, such as recording data in a secure and immutable manner, deploying censorship-resistant smart contracts, and tokenizing digital assets. Taken together, these capabilities have the potential to revolutionize green finance and aid in the global fight against climate change.

To critically evaluate the usefulness and effectiveness of blockchain technologies in combating climate change, several factors need to be considered. First, for blockchain technology to be adopted to tackle climate change, its potential benefits must outweigh the energy consumption required to power the technology. Energy consumption is a concern because it contributes to greenhouse gas emissions; computers used on the blockchain are powered by fossil fuels, which release greenhouse gases into the atmosphere, contributing to global warming and other environmental problems. In fact, high consumption of energy is one of the major criticisms of blockchain technology and must be considered when evaluating its usefulness in addressing climate change.[10] Second, blockchain technology

---

[9]As noted by Hileman and Rauchs (2017), not all blockchains are created to be equal. The security and effectiveness of a blockchain depends on various factors such as the level of decentralization and openness, as well as the consensus mechanism used by participating nodes. Decentralized and public blockchains are the technologies of choice for ReFi. They typically provide relatively higher security for recorded transactions but may experience issues with efficiency (scalability). In contrast, centralized blockchains have greater efficiency, but may not offer the same level of security, as determined by the blockchain trilemma principle (Touloupou *et al.*, 2022).

[10]Blockchain technology consumes a high amount of energy because significant computational resources are required to validate and process transactions on the blockchain. This validation process requires powerful computers to compete against one another to solve a complex mathematical

needs to be scalable to effectively handle large amounts of data. The ability to increase the number of transactions that can be processed without compromising security or transaction speed is important for blockchain technology to become widely adopted. If the network cannot keep up with the increasing demand, it could not only lead to slow processing time, higher transaction fees, and reduced efficiency, but also become centralized as users are forced to rely on a limited number of nodes to process transactions. Scalability has been a significant challenge for blockchain technology. The current blockchain infrastructure may not be able to meet the needs of the global community in addressing climate change, particularly for public blockchains such as Bitcoin and Ethereum, which have limited transaction processing capacities.[11]

Third, for blockchain technology to help mitigate the effects of climate change, it must be transparent to ensure that climate-related applications are effective and reliable. For example, carbon trading aims to reduce greenhouse gas emissions through the buying and selling of carbon credits.[12] Blockchain technology

---

puzzle, known as "proof of work"; the computer that solves the puzzle first is then given authority to add the next block of transactions to the blockchain. Therefore, the more powerful the computer, the more quickly it can solve these calculations and validate transactions, but the more energy it consumes. To add on, the decentralized nature of the validation process implies that numerous computers and nodes within the network must collaborate to validate and authenticate transactions, leading to a significant amount of energy consumption. That said, there are efforts underway to develop energy-efficient consensus mechanisms, such as proof of stake, that do not rely on computational puzzles and renewable energy sources such as solar or wind power to power mining rigs.

[11]There are ongoing efforts to address scalability issues. Some proposed solutions include sharding, Layer 2 solutions, proof of stake, off-chain transactions, and block size increase. For example, sharding has been proposed as a solution to overcome the scalability issues of Ethereum; the blockchain is divided into smaller parts called shards, each of which can process transactions independently. The parallel processing of transactions can significantly increase the network's throughput, enabling Ethereum to process more transactions per second, compared to the current limit of 15–45 transactions per second.

[12]These credits are regarded as a commodity that permits an entity to emit a certain amount of greenhouse gases. The system of carbon trading originated from the Kyoto Protocol, a United Nations treaty that was written to mitigate the contribution of greenhouse gases to climate change. As a certification authority inspects controlled companies, an emission baseline is set for the industry, in which each company gets allocated an emission allowance. Companies that are able to reduce their emissions due to successful energy-saving transformation or technology upgrade enjoy a surplus in carbon emissions, which can be sold to companies which have exceeded their emission quota. In this way, companies are incentivized to cut back on their emissions so that they have leftover emission permits to sell. Higher-polluting companies which have exceeded their emission quota are also able to buy the surplus emission. The end result of this "cap and trade" initiative is controlled carbon emissions and a big step towards decarbonization (Bumpus and Liverman, 2008).

enables these credits to be traded using digital tokens and accelerates the development of peer-to-peer (P2P) carbon trading to support climate initiatives. A blockchain that is transparent allows for the creation of a tamper-proof ledger of carbon credits on the network. It also facilitates transparent carbon trading by eliminating the problem of double counting carbon emissions. This prevents greenwashing and builds trust and accountability in the carbon credit market (Marchant *et al.*, 2022). As stakeholders can verify and track the source and transfer of carbon credit, they are assured that these credits are valid and being used appropriately.[13] Moreover, carbon trading on blockchain eliminates the need for a central authority to oversee the transactions and enables a decentralized approach to the trading of carbon credits, reducing the time for trade clearance and approval.

In fact, the carbon trading process can be further accelerated as negotiation and agreements are digitalized using blockchain-based smart contracts. These contracts offer a self-executing, traceable, and tamper-proof way of calculating, tracking, and disclosing carbon footprint reductions, which could potentially incentivize eco-friendly actions on a global scale (Al Sadawi *et al.*, 2021). Blockchain technology can therefore solve the problems of trust, transparency and security related to climate data processing, thereby helping to mitigate the climate crisis by promoting sustainable growth in the global economy. Additionally, it creates a more accessible and efficient carbon market through asset tokenization, whereby bulk carbon credit financial instruments are broken down into smaller units so that individual investors and companies can play a part in creating a carbon-neutral future (Saraji and Borowczak, 2021; Dorfleitner and Braun, 2019). Notably, tokenization further enhances transparency and traceability in the carbon market as each token represents a specific amount of reduction or removal of carbon emissions. This helps to prevent fraud and ensures that the carbon credits being traded are legitimate and verifiable.

Fourth, for there to be widespread adoption of the technology, different blockchain networks must be able to communicate and interact with one another seamlessly.[14] Even though Ethereum is still the most extensively utilized public blockchain, other emerging platforms like Binance, Polkadot, Algorand, and

[13]The immutability of data recorded on open, public and decentralized blockchains highlights the incorruptible nature of this technology and its ability to act as a trust enhancing machine (Berg *et al.*, 2017). With no central authority controlling the transactions, credibility and accountability of recorded data are enhanced by cryptography as participants of the P2P network rely on hashing algorithms and message digests to ensure the integrity of the transactions.

[14]Blockchain platforms designed for specific uses often operate in isolation from one another. This can result in fragmentation and inefficiencies, thereby limiting the potential benefits of blockchain technology.

Cardano are gaining popularity rapidly. As such, enabling seamless communication and exchange of assets among different blockchain platforms is important in achieving climate change goals. A major challenge resides in the need for blockchain technology to be standardized and interoperable, particularly in the context of sustainability. Effective technological interoperability among diverse blockchain platforms is, however, still in its experimental stage (Kang *et al.*, 2022). Last, the adoption of blockchain technology to combat climate change depends on the stakeholders' level of interest and support, which is affected by their education level, the amount of funding available, and the regulatory and legal framework in place (Sheldon, 2021; Pasdar *et al.*, 2022). In fact, the regulation of blockchains and digital assets is still locally diverse, fragmented, and in many cases, lacking altogether, therefore slowing down the global adoption of blockchain technology (Malhotra *et al.*, 2022).

In sum, although blockchain technology has the potential to be a powerful tool to support sustainability efforts, it is not a silver bullet solution for addressing climate change. Other strategies such as transitioning to renewable energy sources, improving energy efficiency, and implementing carbon pricing policies are also necessary to achieve meaningful progress towards a more sustainable future. Nevertheless, the technology offers a new approach to managing and tracking environmental assets to incentivize sustainable behavior and foster collaboration across stakeholders. Along with policy and market reforms in place to create the right incentives for stakeholders to adopt sustainable practices, blockchain technology can create a more sustainable future for generations to come.

3.2. *Artificial intelligence*

AI is an important tool to fight climate change. When used responsibly, it can significantly improve the assessment of greenhouse gas emissions, and increase energy efficiency, especially renewably sourced. In general, AI refers to the development of computer systems to perform tasks that normally require human intelligence. AI algorithms can empower the computational analysis of big data to reveal recurring weather patterns, hence improving the predictability of extreme weather events and providing the necessary decision-making tools to respond to these climate changes effectively. For example, AI can process several pictures, graphs, and maps to analyze the sea level rise and ice sheet. A high-resolution radar network with satellite data and high-altitude weather balloons can help to improve the forecasting power of existing weather networks. In a process known as machine learning, AI recognizes and internalizes patterns and images. As computers sort through a large amount of data, the algorithms recognize specific elements and provide recommendations or solutions, mimicking and improving human decision-making. In fact, AI technology can, at a speed faster than any human, review thousands of photographs of the aftermath of a hurricane and determine which trees have been destroyed.

Overall, AI and machine learning can be particularly effective in fighting climate change by improving the understanding of the environmental impact of human activities, predicting potential climate change effects, and identifying solutions that can mitigate these effects. These technologies can process vast amounts of data and identify patterns and trends that may be difficult or impossible for humans to discern. Through such analysis, valuable insights about the complex environmental systems can be obtained and applied to make informed decisions on how to adapt to the changing climate. For example, machine learning algorithms can be used to improve the accuracy of climate prediction models by identifying patterns and trends in historical climate data and using that information to improve the models' predictions about future climate trends. They can also be used to identify the best locations for carbon capture and determine the most efficient ways to transport and store carbon. The production and distribution of renewable energy, such as wind and solar, can also be optimized by AI and machine learning to predict energy demand and manage energy storage.

There are also multiple approaches through which AI and machine learning can contribute to the reduction of greenhouse gas emissions. First, AI-enabled vehicles can identify the most energy-efficient routes and minimize energy usage. These vehicles are fully autonomous and require no human involvement. Road hazards can be communicated among these vehicles, which reduces the number of accidents on the road. Second, AI is able to accurately identify weather changes and tropical cyclones. Compared to meteorologists, AI can anticipate heat waves and other extreme weather events with greater accuracy. This enables people to better prepare for extreme weather conditions and minimize weather risks. Third, farmers can tap into AI technology to reduce the loss of freshwater due to poor resource management. AI enables farmers to irrigate crops efficiently, thereby reducing the waste of fresh water through numerous sprinkler heads. The use of fertilizers and scheduling of planting seasons can also be optimized with AI, resulting in higher yields from farming fields. Fourth, AI improves urban planning as it makes a city more efficient and increases the quality of life. In fact, in an AI-supported "smart city", the waste of resources is reduced as the use of water and energy is optimized. The technology also facilitates a faster response to disasters as it can quickly process information and direct resources to the most needed channels following extreme weather events. Last, AI can provide greater access to information by analyzing satellite imageries and processing visual information with great speed. This enables governments to monitor the environmental protection efforts of their countries and enhances consumers' understanding about the environmental impact of their consumption behavior.

While AI presents many technological innovations to combat the effects of climate change, it is not without its limitations. The technology can harm the environment and contribute to global warming as it requires rare minerals such as cobalt, lithium and tantalum, the extraction of which can impose significant environmental costs; the mining of waste from tantalum extraction pollutes local water resources. In addition, training AI models consumes a massive amount of energy, resulting in significant carbon emissions from large data farms and processing centers. Electronic waste and toxic substances such as mercury are also produced in the process, which can leak into the environment and increase global temperature. As a result, environmental policymakers need to evaluate the areas in which AI can outperform existing technologies and how AI can be used to tackle climate change without adding burden to the environment through carbon emissions.

3.3. *Other innovative technologies and business models*

IoT, big data, and crowdfunding platforms are related and complementary technologies that can work alongside blockchain and AI to achieve green finance objectives (Ignatyuk *et al.*, 2020; Jha *et al.*, 2022; Nassiry, 2019). IoT is a vast network of sensor devices that can collect information from the environment and communicate not only with the main data processing computer, but also with one another. When incorporated with machine learning, IoT becomes an incredibly powerful tool; through the application of machine learning algorithms, massive amounts of data generated by IoT devices can be analyzed to detect climate patterns and anomalies and obtain valuable insights about weather changes, natural disasters, and other environmental factors. For example, financial institutions can use IoT sensors to monitor environmental parameters such as energy consumption, air quality, water usage, and waste generation, and develop targeted green finance solutions. IoT sensors can also be used to monitor the energy usage of buildings, allowing financial institutions to develop financing solutions that promote energy efficiency. By collecting and analyzing real-time data, financial institutions can make more informed decisions that contribute to sustainability.

With the advancement of the digital economy, the amount of data generated is growing at an unprecedented rate. Big data analytics is playing an increasingly important role in helping organizations to understand and address climate change issues. By leveraging the vast amounts of data generated by IoT sensors and other sources, businesses can gain valuable insights into climate patterns, identify potential risks, and develop effective strategies to mitigate the impact of climate change. For example, big data analytics can help businesses measure their carbon footprint and assess the environmental impact of their operations. By gathering and analyzing data on energy consumption, waste generation, and other environmental factors, businesses can identify areas where they can reduce their environmental impact and implement more sustainable practices.

Green crowdfunding platforms represent a collaboration between fintech and sustainable finance in that they leverage financial innovation and technology to democratize access to finance, facilitating the mobilization of capital towards environmentally friendly projects.[15] These platforms promote financial inclusion by operating on the crowdfunding principle of raising small sums of money from a wide audience, which might not have been achievable through traditional financing methods such as venture capital or bank loans. Eco-friendly project creators such as individuals and organizations can showcase their ideas on the platforms and appeal to the audience for funding. In this way, the playing field is leveled as everyone has an equal opportunity to receive financial support from a more diverse group of online users. Blockchain-based crowdfunding platforms like Ethereum can automate the investment process and reduce transaction costs, making it easy and cost-effective to invest in green projects. By utilizing blockchain technology, these platforms can automate various stages of the investment process, including payment processing, record-keeping, and distribution of rewards to investors. In fact, with the use of smart contracts, these platforms can automate the entire investment process, thereby reducing the need for intermediaries and lowering transaction costs. This automation makes it easy not only for investors to participate in eco-friendly projects, but also for project creators to access a broad pool of potential investors.

4. Governance in Green Finance and Green Fintech

As with any industry, there are potential ethical issues associated with green finance and green fintech. To ensure that investments in environmentally friendly projects are made in an ethical manner, it is crucial to have effective governance

[15] Several examples of green crowdfunding platforms include Abundance in the UK, Ecomill in Italy, and Lendosphere in France, each promoting investments in renewable energy projects, low-carbon electricity, low-environmental impact projects, and loans for enterprises in the renewable energy sector (Chueca Vergara and Ferruz Agudo, 2021).

in place for green finance and green fintech.[16] In green finance, ethical considerations focus on ensuring that investments are environmentally friendly and in line with the sustainability goals which they set out to achieve. In green fintech, ethical considerations emphasize the creation of financial technological products and services that promote not only environmental sustainability and social responsibility, but also financial inclusion. Governance in green finance and green fintech involves establishing policies, practices and regulations that promote transparency, accountability, and sustainability across the financial industry. This includes ensuring that environmental and social risks are identified and addressed, and investments are aligned with sustainability goals. In transitioning towards a sustainable economy, it is important that the potential benefits of green finance and green fintech be realized in an ethical and responsible way. In doing so, ethical issues such as green washing, bias and discrimination, environmental justice, data privacy and security, need to be addressed.

Greenwashing has become increasingly prevalent in recent years. As consumers become more environmentally conscious, more companies are attempting to portray themselves as being environmentally friendly when they are not. For example, companies can make false or exaggerated claims about the environmental benefits of their products, such as using ambiguous or difficult-to-verify language or highlighting minor environmental features while downplaying significant environmental issues. As such, greenwashing not only misleads consumers who care about the environment and want to make informed choices, but also undermines the efforts of genuinely environmentally responsible companies to make a positive impact on the environment. To address greenwashing, policymakers and regulators need to develop clear standards for environmental claims, including definitions and requirements for terms such as "eco-friendly" or "green". Penalties, such as fines or sanctions, should also be enforced upon companies that are found to have engaged in deceptive marketing practices. Consumers also need to be equipped with tools to verify the authenticity of environmental claims to make more informed purchasing decisions. By taking a comprehensive approach to address greenwashing, companies can build consumer trust, which can lead to increased demand for sustainable products and services, that can in turn drive innovation in the field of sustainability.

Bias and discrimination can also be significant ethical issues in green finance and green fintech. Algorithm-based systems can perpetuate biases if they are

---

[16] Governance refers to the structures, processes, and policies that are put in place to regulate green finance and green fintech to ensure that the interests of all stakeholders, including investors, issuers, regulators, and the society as a whole, are taken into account.

trained on historical data, which does not consider the experiences of underrepresented groups.[17] Biases can also occur when algorithms, which do not fully consider the social or environmental contexts of different communities, are used to assess environmental risks.[18] To address these biases, green fintech tools should be developed with a diverse range of perspectives and inputs. This may involve considering the experiences of underrepresented groups in the financial system, as well as constantly monitoring and evaluating these tools to ensure that they do not perpetuate existing biases. In using algorithms to assess environmental risks, a range of society and environmental factors[19] should be considered to capture the full extent of the risks more accurately. By mitigating the bias and discrimination that can occur in the realm of green finance and green fintech, sustainable financing opportunities can become available to everyone, regardless of their background or identity. This promotes equal access to green financial products and services, which can drive investments towards environmentally friendly projects.

Data privacy and security is another ethical concern that is crucial in maintaining trust in green finance and green fintech. As green fintech companies collect an increasing amount of personal data to provide their services, it is essential that this data be stored in a secure and ethical manner and there is no misuse or unauthorized access to sensitive information. In conclusion, effective governance of green finance and green fintech is critical for promoting environmentally friendly investments and ensuring that they contribute to global efforts to mitigate climate change. However, there are significant challenges to achieving such effective governance. To address these challenges, it is crucial to have transparency and accountability in green finance and green fintech. Financial institutions and fintech companies must provide transparent information about the environmental and social impact of their products and services and be accountable for the impact of their investments and financial products. It is also essential to accurately measure and report the impact so that investors and customers can assess the true

[17]For example, a green fintech tool that depends on algorithms to evaluate the eligibility of businesses for green loans may be biased if the tool is trained on past lending patterns that discriminated against minority-owned businesses or businesses in underserved communities. As a result, businesses owned by underrepresented groups of people are unjustly denied access to green finance, further exacerbating existing inequalities.

[18]For example, algorithms may not fully capture the risk of wildfires faced by communities that are living in fire-prone areas because the risk assessment is based only on data about vegetation or climate conditions. Areas with a high density of dry vegetation may not be at high risk of wildfires if the communities living in the areas have effective fire prevention measures in place.

[19]This includes information on housing density, population density, socioeconomic factors, and other community-specific data that can affect environmental risks.

sustainability of their investments and make informed decisions. Environmental and social due diligence must also be conducted before investments are made or new financial products and services are launched. Moreover, green finance and green fintech should be designed to promote financial inclusion and reduce inequalities. They should be guided by environmental and social standards to ensure that minimum environmental and social requirements are met.[20]

5. Green Technology Success Stories: Real-Life Examples of Climate Change Mitigation and Sustainability Achievement

Green technology has become increasingly important in mitigating climate change. Through innovative solutions, businesses and organizations have been able to reduce their environmental impact, while also driving economic growth and creating new opportunities for sustainable development. In this section, we will highlight some real-life examples of green technology success stories, showcasing the different ways in which businesses and organizations are using technology to achieve sustainability goals. These case studies have been selected based on their relevance to the topics covered, their established position in the markets and their ability to illustrate key points in a clear and concise manner. Most of them are from the Singaporean market, one of the most transparent and regulated market supporting these technologies (Lin, 2019; MAS, 2022).

5.1. *Bringing carbon trading to traditional commodity exchanges*

The existence of a market for trading carbon credits facilitates the achievement of the carbon neutrality goal. Financial technologies play an important role in turning carbon into a commodity that can be readily traded to ease the emission of greenhouse gases. Various fintech inter-related projects have emerged over the years to offer different ways of achieving this goal by focusing on such aspects of the market as the ability to trade carbon on exchanges, meeting different trading needs, and verifying carbon data. Blockchain and AI play key roles in this process. Additionally, ReFi projects emphasize the decentralized nature of governance models and their ability to address issues with voluntary carbon markets (VCMs).

[20] These include international standards such as the UN Sustainable Development Goals and the Paris Agreement on climate change.

Blockchain technology can be used to increase the efficiency of carbon trading and make market access less exclusive by empowering individuals and small companies to trade carbon credits.

AirCarbon Exchange (n.d.) is a Singapore-based carbon trading platform, backed by the country's government agency known as the Enterprise Development Fund. It is a global trading platform for carbon credits that leverages blockchain technology to allow buyers and sellers to trade these credits in a secure and transparent manner. Securitizing carbon credits converts the right to release a specific amount of CO_2 into tradable digital tokens that live on the blockchain. For every such token, the exchange holds one carbon credit as a deposit, which represents the removal of 1 ton of carbon dioxide equivalent (tCO_2e) from the atmosphere. Therefore, individuals and organizations can buy these tokens to support environmental initiatives. The tokenization process improves liquidity in the carbon markets and promotes climate change efforts by using digital currencies backed by carbon assets. Using a distributed ledger, the carbon marketplace enables carbon credits to be traded in a frictionless and transparent manner, ensuring that carbon removal is accurately measured (Velezmoro, 2022).

5.2. *Meeting different carbon trading needs*

Climate Impact X (2022) is a Singapore-based carbon exchange that uses satellite monitoring, machine learning and blockchain technology to increase the transparency, integrity, and quality of carbon credits. It consists of three digital platforms, namely the carbon exchange, project marketplace, and auction. The carbon exchange caters to larger-scale buyers, such as multinational corporations and institutional investors, and trades carbon contracts which set out standardized terms and conditions under which carbon credits are traded. Hence, these contracts enable a high volume of standardized carbon credits to be pooled together across multiple projects. On the other hand, the project marketplace serves a different buyer need by specializing in high-quality carbon credits from specific natural climate solutions (NCS) projects with different business missions and sustainability priorities (Tan, 2022). The auction platform entails an interactive and transparent bidding process that facilitates competitive price discovery (Liau, 2022). As such, it is targeted at suppliers with large-scale or new-to-market carbon credits.

5.3. *Generating global carbon trading flows*

MetaVerse Green Exchange (MVGX) is a digital green exchange that strives to create a sustainable and green future in the metaverse era (MVG, n.d.). Specifically, it aims to provide green and sustainable financing to large corporations to help them achieve carbon neutrality. For example, to offset their carbon emissions, companies can buy Carbon Neutrality Tokens, which are tokenized carbon credits supported by a distributed ledger technology that maintains a verifiable and immutable record of the carbon performance of all assets on the trading platform. By buying the carbon credits, investors are effectively investing in green projects and taking a step towards future decarbonization. These green digital assets are essentially the bridge between green investments in traditional finance and the global carbon trading markets.

5.4. *Verifying carbon data*

To tackle climate change, carbon emissions need to be accurately measured and responsibly accounted for. Corporate carbon reporting can be inaccurate because not all data can be proven legitimate as they cannot be independently verified. As a result, there is a lack of transparency and a certain level of distrust in the carbon emission data. VeChain is a smart contract-compatible blockchain platform designed to enhance business processes.[21] To overcome the difficulty of verifying carbon data, it initiated a digital footprint software-as-a-service (SaaS) platform that enables businesses to redesign their carbon footprint data management practices. Specifically, VeCarbon is a blockchain-based SaaS that assists enterprises to better calculate, track and report their carbon emissions, thereby helping them to achieve carbon neutrality and sustainability goals.[22] When combined with IoT technologies and data quality assurance, blockchain is able to collect carbon emission data from numerous participants of a supply chain in a trustless manner. The interconnectedness of the blockchain enables users to record key data on the blockchain and integrate it with third-party assurance providers within the partnership network. In this way, business entities provide end users with the full set of carbon data, which can change the way consumers view carbon labelling and alter their consumption behavior.

5.5. *Tracking carbon emissions and tracing carbon production*

The Wantan Rubik's Cube Blockchain Low-Carbon Service Platform by Wanxiang Blockchain empowers companies to achieve the dual-carbon goals with its

[21] See VeChain Foundation (n.d.), Coinbase (n.d.), and Kroeger (2021).

[22] See VeChain Carbon (n.d.), VeChain Foundation (2021a, 2021b), and Crypto News Flash (2022a, 2022b).

one-stop dual-carbon digital management tool which consists of multiple technologies such as blockchain, security cloud, knowledge graph, IoT, and AI. That is, blockchain provides the underlying trusted data infrastructure, secure cloud computing guarantees the security of the data connection and knowledge graph provides the algorithms for calculating carbon emissions (Wanxiang Blockchain, 2021). Together, these technical integrations protect data rights, ensure that carbon economy-related parts are reliably circulated and credibly confirm the carbon emission measurements associated with the carbon assets. Enterprises are therefore able to monitor product life cycle carbon footprints, track the carbon emissions of buildings and parks, and reliably trace, analyze and supervise carbon assets.

5.6. *Smart contracting*

In today's rapidly changing business landscape, companies are increasingly being held accountable for their impact on the environment, society, and corporate governance. This has led to the emergence of the concept of Environmental, Social, and Governance (ESG) goals, which are a set of ethical standards that businesses must meet to be considered socially responsible. While achieving these goals can be a complex and challenging task, companies can leverage technology to accelerate their progress towards achieving their ESG objectives. Vetta is an end-to-end smart contract platform that interacts with companies' ESG data, receives ongoing notifications of the key life cycle events of these companies and executes the required actions automatically.[23] In this way, companies can more easily obtain ESG financing as the environmental impact of their projects can be indisputably measured using blockchain technology. Moreover, they can also earn a secondary stream of income by trading on high-quality carbon credits made possible by the blockchain-based carbon trading platform. In fact, the platform provides an efficient and affordable way to obtain certified carbon credits and lowers the barrier of entry for both corporate entities and consumers.

However, it is important to note that smart contracts can operate not only on open, public, and decentralized blockchains, but also on legacy systems that lack the advantages of decentralization. In such scenarios, ReFi's dedication to decentralization can provide viable solutions. Although ReFi recognizes that many organizations still rely on traditional systems that are not fully decentralized, these systems can still benefit from the use of smart contracts to automate and

[23] See STACS (n.d.) and FinTech News Singapore (2022).

streamline business processes. Specifically, smart contracts can reduce the risk of errors and fraud, increase efficiency, and enhance transparency, even within legacy systems. To achieve this, ReFi projects utilize decentralized platforms that allow businesses to leverage the power of smart contracts within their existing infrastructure. By using ReFi's platform, companies can benefit from the security and transparency of decentralized systems, without having to overhaul their entire technology stack. Therefore, businesses can more easily adopt decentralized solutions and enjoy the benefits of a more transparent and efficient business model.

5.7. *Matching carbon credits in VCM with ReFi's DAO model*

By choosing to build its applications on the most open and widely used blockchain platforms, such as Ethereum and Celo, the approach of ReFi demonstrates a commitment to transparency and decentralization that benefits a large population. This ensures that ReFi's solutions are accessible to a broad range of users, promoting transparency and fairness in the financial system. However, open global and decentralized projects face the challenge of maintaining sustainable and collaborative communities due to the problem of voluntary contribution mechanisms (VCMs), which is also described by Ostrom's "problem of managing the commons" (Walljasper, 2011).[24] Diaz-Valdivia and Poblet (2022) examine how projects, like KlimaDAO, use the DAO governance model to implement various mechanisms, such as token-based rewards and penalties, distributed decision-making, and dynamic funding mechanism, to incentivize cooperation and collective action among the community members.

KlimaDAO is a DAO, consisting of a group of environmentalists, developers and entrepreneurs that aim to use blockchain technology to accelerate the trading of carbon credits (KlimaDAO, n.d.). The trading platform enables Web3 builders

[24] VCM refers to the challenge of motivating individuals to contribute to the maintenance and development of a shared resource. This challenge is particularly acute in the context of open, global and decentralized projects because individuals often do not have a direct stake in the project or may not feel a sense of ownership or responsibility. The "problem of managing the commons" refers to the difficulty of designing institutional arrangements and governance structures that enable individuals to collectively manage and sustainably use a common-pool resource. To successfully manage commons, it is necessary to have in place, a combination of formal rules, informal norms, and social capital to encourage individuals to work toward towards a common goal. Therefore, to address the challenge of VCM, there needs to be a similar combination of institutional arrangements, norms, and incentives to encourage community involvement and contribution, which may include the use of token incentives, community governance structures, and social norms that promote collaboration and ownership among project participants.

and users to trade carbon through its native token, known as the Klima. The token is a cryptocurrency whose value is linked to carbon credits. In other words, the token can only be minted if it is backed by tokenized carbon credits. In fact, since the launch of the VCM in October 2021, KlimaDAO has matched 17,000,000 tons of carbon credits to its tokens. This makes the market for Klima tokens more accessible to everyone compared to the current VCM, which can take months to source for carbon credits and work with a brokerage firm to retire these credits. In fact, anyone can trade Klima tokens without needing a third-party broker to source for or offset carbon.

6. Conclusion

Climate change is an urgent and pressing issue that demands immediate attention and action. The need to mitigate the effects of climate change and achieve carbon neutrality has become more critical than ever before. Without a collective global effort that involves taking actions in the environmental, social, and economic dimensions, the impacts of climate change are likely to worsen, leading to irreversible damage to the planet and its inhabitants. As such, it is essential that we prioritize climate action and work towards a sustainable future for all. To combat climate change within the economic dimension, green finance and ReFi, along with technological innovations such as blockchain, AI, IoT, big data analytics, and crowdfunding platforms have emerged as promising tools to advance sustainable development and address the environmental challenges.

As these financial technologies evolve rapidly, their applications are becoming increasingly prevalent in the fight against climate change. With the use of green technologies and approaches, the environmental impacts of economic activities such as carbon footprints and greenhouse gas emissions, can be accurately measured and tracked to promote environmental efforts and actions, which contribute to a net-zero carbon future. The real-life case studies presented in this paper demonstrate the tangible benefits of adopting green technologies in achieving sustainability goals and mitigating the impacts of climate change.

The future of finance lies in the promotion of sustainable practices, and green fintech plays a critical role in enabling this transition. As such, it is crucial that financial institutions embrace sustainable finance practices and integrate green fintech solutions into their operations to support the transition to a more sustainable and equitable future. In doing so, financial institutions must operate with a strong ethical foundation and adhere to relevant laws, regulations, and standards. For, the governance aspects of sustainable finance and green fintech are essential in ensuring that environmental and social responsibilities are upheld. By prioritizing ethics and compliance, financial institutions can build trust with their stakeholders such as customers, investors, and the wider community; trust can foster cooperation among stakeholders and lead to more effective and efficient environmental efforts as they work together to mitigate the effects of climate change.

In sum, this paper explores the emerging fields of green finance, ReFi, and green fintech. These areas of finance represent important opportunities to mobilize capital towards environmentally sustainable and socially responsible investments. By redirecting financial flows towards sustainable projects and investments, green finance has the potential to drive the transition to a low-carbon economy. In contrast, ReFi goes beyond sustainable development by seeking to restore natural capital and foster better ecosystem health. Green fintech, on the other hand, transforms the financial industry by improving the efficiency and transparency of investments, while also enabling new forms of impact measurement and reporting. As the momentum towards greener finance grows, these technologies and approaches can help address urgent environmental and social challenges, thereby creating a more positive future for all.

References

AirCarbon Exchange, n.d., About, AirCarbon Exchange, https://www.aircarbon.co/about-aircarbon.

Al Sadawi, A., B. Madani, S. Saboor, M. Ndiaye, and G. Abu-Lebdeh, 2021, A Comprehensive Hierarchical Blockchain System for Carbon Emission Trading Utilizing Blockchain of Things and Smart Contract, *Technological Forecasting and Social Change* 173, 121124.

Assembly, G., 2015, Resolution Adopted by the General Assembly on 11 September 2015, United Nations, New York.

Azil, A., and J. Sengupta, 2022, Fostering Fintech in Green Finance: An Interview with Sopnendu Mohanty [Interview], McKinsey & Company, https://www.mckinsey.com/featured-insights/future-of-asia/videos/fostering-fintech-in-green-finance-an-interview-with-sopnendu-mohanty.

Bel, G., and S. Joseph, 2018, Climate Change Mitigation and the Role of Technological Change: Impact on Selected Headline Targets of Europe's 2020 Climate and Energy Package, *Renewable and Sustainable Energy Reviews* 82, 3798–3807.

Berg, C., S. Davidson, and J. Potts, 2017, Blockchains Industrialise Trust (November 19, 2017). Available at SSRN: http://dx.doi.org/10.2139/ssrn.3074070.

BloombergNEF, 2022, Global New Investment in Renewable Energy in H1 2022 Reaches $226bn, BloombergNEF, https://about.bnef.com/blog/renewable-energy-sector-defies-supply-chain-challenges-to-hit-a-record-first-half-for-new-investment/.

Bumpus, A. G., and D. M. Liverman, 2008, Accumulation by Decarbonization and the Governance of Carbon Offsets, *Economic Geography* 84(2), 127–155.

Chueca Vergara, C., and L. Ferruz Agudo, 2021, Fintech and Sustainability: Do They Affect Each Other? *Sustainability* 13(13), 7012.

Climate Impact X, n.d., https://www.climateimpactx.com.

Coinbase, n.d., VeChain Price, Coinbase, https://www.coinbase.com/price/vechain.

Crypto News Flash, 2022a, Big News for VeChain: VeCarbon Has Received Highest Level of Protection, https://www.crypto-news-flash.com/big-news-for-vechain-vecarbon-has-received-highest-level-of-protection/.

Crypto News Flash, 2022b, VeChain Reduces Carbon Emission by 95%, Will It Drive VET to $1? https://www.crypto-news-flash.com/vechain-reduces-carbon-emission-by-95-will-it-drive-vet-to-1/.

Diaz-Valdivia, A., and M. Poblet, 2022, Governance of ReFi Ecosystem and the Integrity of Voluntary Carbon Markets as a Common Resource, SSRN 4286167.

Dorfleitner, G., and D. Braun, 2019, Fintech, Digitalization and Blockchain: Possible Applications for Green Finance, in M. Migliorelli, and P. Dessertine (editors), *The Rise of Green Finance in Europe*, Palgrave Studies in Impact Finance, Palgrave Macmillan, Cham, https://doi.org/10.1007/978-3-030-22510-0_9.

FinTech News Singapore, 2022, STACS Launches Its Full Suite of ESG Solutions in Sustainable Finance Push, Retrieved March 1, 2023, https://fintechnews.sg/59806/blockchain/stacs-launches-its-full-suite-of-esg-solutions-in-sustainable-finance-push/.

Fullerton, J., 2015, *Regenerative Capitalism*, Capital Institute, Greenwich, CT, USA.

Hileman, G., and M. Rauchs, 2017, Global Blockchain Benchmarking Study, https://www.jbs.cam.ac.uk/wp-content/uploads/2020/08/2017-09-27-ccaf-globalbchain.pdf.

Ignatyuk, A., O. Liubkina, T. Murovana, and A. Magomedova, 2020, FinTech as an Innovation Challenge: From Big Data to Sustainable Development, *E3S Web of Conferences* 166, 13027.

Jha, B., P. Giri, D. Jha, and U. Badhera, 2022, Unlocking IoT: AI-Enabled Green FinTech Innovations, in *AI-Enabled Agile Internet of Things for Sustainable FinTech Ecosystems*, IGI Global, Hershey, PA, pp. 1–22.

Jiang, J., W. Wang, C. Wang, and Y. Liu, 2017, Combating Climate Change Calls for a Global Technological Cooperation System Built on the Concept of Ecological Civilization, *Chinese Journal of Population Resources and Environment* 15(1), 21–31.

Kang, I., A. Gupta, and O. Seneviratne, 2022, Blockchain Interoperability Landscape, arXiv:2212.09227.

KlimaDAO, n.d., KlimaDAO, Retrieved March 1, 2023, https://www.klimadao.finance/.

Kroeger, L., 2021, What is VeChain (VET) and How Does It Work? Cointelegraph, https://cointelegraph.com/news/what-is-vechain-vet-and-how-does-it-work.

Liau, C., 2022, First Major Carbon Credit Auction by Singapore-Based Climate Impact X Oversubscribed, *The Straits Times*, https://www.straitstimes.com/business/first-major-carbon-credit-auction-by-singapore-based-climate-impact-x-oversubscribed.

Li, M., and Q. Wang, 2017, Will Technology Advances Alleviate Climate Change? Dual Effects of Technology Change on Aggregate Carbon Dioxide Emissions, *Energy for Sustainable Development* 41, 61–68.

Lin, L., 2019, Regulating FinTech: The Case of Singapore, *SSRN Electronic Journal* 35, 94–119, http://dx.doi.org/10.2139/ssrn.3481563.

Malhotra, A., H. O'Neill, and P. Stowell, 2022, Thinking Strategically About Blockchain Adoption and Risk Mitigation, *Business Horizons* 65(2), 159–171.

Marchant, G. E., Z. Cooper, and P. J. Gough-Stone, 2022, Bringing Technological Transparency to Tenebrous Markets: The Case for Using Blockchain to Validate Carbon Credit Trading Markets, *Natural Resources Journal* 62, 159.

MAS, 2022, FinTech Regulatory Sandbox Guidelines (January 2022), https://www.mas.gov.sg/-/media/MAS-Media-Library/development/Regulatory-Sandbox/Sandbox/FinTech-Regulatory-Sandbox-Guidelines-Jan-2022.pdf?la=en&hash=0136A576014D8B13D16264CDFDA2C66791F6E8CA.

MAS, n.d., Green Fintech, https://www.mas.gov.sg/development/fintech/Green-FinTech.

MVG, n.d., Carbon Offset Projects, MVG, https://www.mvgx.com.

Nassiry, D., 2019, The Role of Fintech in Unlocking Green Finance, in *Handbook of Green Finance*, Springer, Singapore, pp. 315–336.

Pasdar, A., Y. C. Lee, and Z. Dong, 2022, Connect API with Blockchain: A Survey on Blockchain Oracle Implementation, *ACM Computing Surveys* 55, 1–39.

Saraji, S., and M. Borowczak, 2021, A Blockchain-Based Carbon Credit Ecosystem, arXiv:2107.00185.

Sheldon, M. D., 2021, Preparing Auditors for the Blockchain Oracle Problem, *Current Issues in Auditing* 15(2), P27–P39.

STACS, n.d., Vetta Platform, Retrieved March 1, 2023, https://stacs.io/vetta-platform/.

Tan, A., 2022, Singapore's Climate Impact X Launches Platform to Facilitate Carbon Credit Trade, *The Straits Times*, https://www.straitstimes.com/singapore/environment/singapores-climate-impact-x-launches-platform-to-facilitate-carbon-credit-trade.

Touloupou, M., M. Themistocleous, E. Iosif, and K. Christodoulou, 2022, A Systematic Literature Review Towards a Blockchain Benchmarking Framework, *IEEE Access* 10, 70630–70644.

United Nations Framework Convention on Climate Change, n.d., Action on Climate and SDGs, https://unfccc.int/topics/cooperative-activities-and-sdgs/action-on-climate-and-sdgs.

VeChain Carbon, n.d., Home, https://www.vecarbon.com/home.

VeChain Foundation, n.d., About Us, VeChain, https://www.vechain.org/about/.

VeChain Foundation, 2021a, Amazon Web Services (AWS) Becomes Technology Partner to VeChain Carbon, Enabling International Scale Carbon Management Services, VeChain, https://medium.com/vechain-foundation/amazon-web-services-aws-becomes-technology-partner-to-vecarbon-enabling-inter-national-scale-162fbad6dd39.

VeChain Foundation, 2021b, VeCarbon: A Critical First Step to Realizing Global Decarbonization Efforts, *Medium*, https://medium.com/vechain-foundation/vecarbon-a-critical-first-step-to-realising-global-decarbonisation-efforts-8b29dad4965b.

Velezmoro, S., 2022, AirCarbon Exchange Moves to Standardise Carbon Trading, *FinanceAsia*, https://www.financeasia.com/article/aircarbon-exchange-moves-to-standardise-carbon-trading/480119.

Walljasper, J., 2011, Elinor Ostrom's 8 Principles for Managing a Commons, Working Paper, On the Commons.

Wanxiang Blockchain, 2021, Wanxiang Blockchain Launches CUBE, a Smart Building Carbon Footprint Monitoring System, *Medium*, https://wxblockchain.medium.com/wanxiang-blockchain-launches-cube-a-smart-building-carbon-footprint-monitoring-system-3793825202c4.

Wang, F. *et al.*, 2021, Technologies and Perspectives for Achieving Carbon Neutrality, *The Innovation* 2(4), 100180.

A Commentary on "An In-depth Guide to Cross-chain Protocols under Multi-chain World"

David Kuo Chuen Lee

School of Business, Singapore University of Social Sciences, Singapore
davidkuochuenlee@gmail.com

1. Introduction

The article "An In-Depth Guide to Cross-Chain Protocols under Multi-Chain World" written by Zheng *et al.* (2023) is intended to assist researchers and industry practitioners in comprehending the concepts, advantages, and limitations of cross-chain technologies. The article addresses various topics, including message transmission protocols, leading cross-chain bridges, and other cross-chain applications. Furthermore, this article considers the potential risks and challenges associated with cross-chain protocols and examines the future of cross-chain protocol development.

However, given the rapid advancements in innovation within this field since its initial publication, several notable changes have emerged in cross-chain protocols. In this review, I will highlight the latest trends within the industry.

2. Review

The advent of artificial intelligence, exemplified by ChatGPT, has prompted developers to increasingly utilize AI in the detection of the security of smart contracts. In comparison to the numerous security incidents that occurred during the early days of DeFi, the security of protocols has undergone a notable improvement. The occurrence of security incidents involving cross-chain bridges has reduced. With the emergence of Layer 2 solutions, users frequently transfer assets across different chains. There is a high demand for cross-chain transactions. The homogeneity of cross-chain bridges is relatively high, and users primarily consider the cost and speed of cross-chain transactions. Some cross-chain bridges, such as Mini Bridge, have identified a niche market by offering lower fees for small transactions.

In the past, the prevailing view among industry analysts was that Bitcoin served as a store of value, while Ethereum was the platform for decentralized applications. Nevertheless, the completion of two significant soft fork upgrades by Bitcoin has led to a reevaluation of its role in the industry. The implementation of SegWit and Taproot has rendered the construction of a Bitcoin ecosystem a viable proposition. Consequently, the construction of BTC Layer 2 solutions has emerged as a significant narrative in the crypto industry for 2024. Previously, cross-chain bridges were primarily concerned with facilitating the transfer of assets from Ethereum Layer 1 to Layer 2, or from EVM-compatible to non-EVM ecosystems, with minimal interaction with BTC mainnet assets. At this juncture, projects employing cross-chain protocols to facilitate the transfer of BTC assets to EVM or Solana ecosystems are garnering considerable attention within the industry.

The composability of cross-chain technology is reducing the complexity of utilizing blockchain, thereby improving the user-friendliness of dApp usage. Intent execution networks, exemplified by dappOS, integrate unified accounts and cross-chain technology, thereby enabling users to readily complete transaction intents without concern for the source chain of the funds. It is anticipated that there will be more dApps joining the unified account ecosystem.

As cross-chain interactions become more frequent, the connections between different protocols become closer, thereby demonstrating the advantage of blockchain composability. However, it should be noted that if a wrapped asset encounters a contract vulnerability or if a cross-chain bridge is attacked, the consequences could extend to multiple protocols. The ongoing consideration of enhancing the security of smart contracts, such as the utilization of AI technology or the design of sophisticated game theory mechanisms, is a matter of interest to developers and token economy designers. The investigation of the potential for combining cross-chain technology with other blockchain technologies to create new composability remains an area of ongoing research. The exploration of the potential for cross-chain bridges to facilitate the integration of central bank digital currencies (CBDCs) or other real-world financial products into the domain of decentralized finance (DeFi) represents a topic of significant academic interest.

An In-depth Guide to Cross-chain Protocols under a Multi-chain World*

Jincheng Zheng† and David Kuo Chuen Lee‡

Singapore University of Social Sciences
463 Clementi Road, Singapore 599494, Singapore
†*jzheng@suss.edu.sg*
‡*davidleekc@suss.edu.sg*

Dejun Qian

Chainge Finance, Singapore
dejun.qian@chainge.finance

In 2021, public blockchains have made remarkable progress with the support of investors and developers, ushering in the era of the multi-chain world, which represents a paradigm shift that is unlikely to be reversed. Cross-chain protocols have become an essential infrastructure in this new world, referring to a standardized set of rules and processes that enable the secure transfer of assets or information between different blockchain networks. To help researchers and industry practitioners better understand the concepts, advantages, and limitations of cross-chain technologies, this paper presents a comprehensive guide to cross-chain protocols. We cover a range of topics, including message transmission protocols, leading cross-chain bridges, and other cross-chain applications. Additionally, we discuss potential risks and challenges associated with cross-chain protocols and explore the future of cross-chain protocol development. Our work is intended to offer valuable insights and references for anyone looking to delve deeper into cross-chain protocols, whether they are academic researchers or industry professionals.

Keywords: Cross-chain; multi-chain; interoperability; blockchain; Web3.

*This Chapter was originally published in the *World Scientific Annual Review of Fintech*, Vol. 1, No. 1, doi: 10.1142/S2811004823500033.

†Corresponding author.

1. Introduction

Cross-chain refers to the transfer of assets or information from one blockchain to another. It allows for interoperability between different blockchain networks, enabling them to work together and allowing users to move their assets from one blockchain to another. This can improve the liquidity of assets and increase the overall value of the combined blockchain ecosystem.

A cross-chain protocol is a set of standardized rules and processes that transfer assets or information between different blockchain networks. These protocols define how information is securely transferred from one blockchain to another, ensuring that all participants agree on the data's validity. By establishing a common language and framework for communication, cross-chain protocols enable blockchains to interoperate and collaborate, allowing for the seamless exchange of assets and increasing the overall value of the blockchain ecosystem. Examples of cross-chain protocols include Cosmos' Inter-Blockchain Communication (IBC) protocol and Polkadot's Substrate.

Multi-chain refers to a blockchain architecture that allows multiple independent chains to exist within the same network. In a multi-chain system, each chain operates as a separate entity and can have its consensus mechanism, token, and set of rules. This allows for a high degree of customization and enables each chain to serve a specific purpose or meet the needs of a particular group of users. By having multiple chains within a single network, multi-chain systems can improve scalability, security, and efficiency compared to single-chain systems. Examples of multi-chain systems include Polkadot and Cosmos.

The link between cross-chain protocols and multi-chain systems is that cross-chain protocols enable communication and interoperability between different chains within a multi-chain system.

In a multi-chain system, each chain operates independently, but cross-chain protocols allow them to interact with one another, enabling the transfer of assets, information, and value. This enables multi-chain systems to offer higher degrees of interoperability and scalability compared to single-chain systems.

The importance of cross-chain protocols and multi-chain systems lies in their ability to overcome limitations and challenges faced by single-chain systems, such as scalability issues, limitations in terms of the types of applications that can be built, and difficulties in achieving consensus. By enabling multiple chains to work together, multi-chain systems and cross-chain protocols offer the potential for increased security, scalability, and overall efficiency, as well as enabling new and innovative use cases for blockchain technology.

2. Cross-chain Demand and Cross-chain Concept under the Multi-chain World

The public blockchain ecosystems have undergone significant growth and development over the past years. However, many of these blockchains were created as standalone systems, resulting in a fragmented landscape where users, assets, and dApps are isolated within their respective ecosystems. This fragmentation runs counter to the principles of interoperability and scalability that form the foundation of blockchain technology.

To address this issue, the crypto-community has realized the importance of cross-chain technology and the need for interoperability between different blockchains. This has led to increased exploration and development of cross-chain protocols and solutions to overcome the limitations of isolated blockchain systems and enable greater collaboration and integration between different blockchains.

2.1. *Cross-chain and Cross-layer*

Cross-chain refers to the transfer of information and assets between distinct and independent blockchain networks. Each blockchain has its own ledger, which maintains a record of all transactions and asset transfers within the network. Side chains, separate from the main chain, do not report their ledgers to the main chain but only communicate with it when cross-chain actions are initiated.

On the other hand, cross-layer refers to the transfer of information and assets between different layers of the same blockchain network. For example, assets are moved from layer 1 to layer 2, or vice versa. In a cross-layer transfer, the bookkeeping unit remains the same, and the transferred information is recorded on the same ledger. Layer 2 solutions, which operate as an extension of the main chain, regularly inform the main chain of updates.

It is important to note that while cross-chain and cross-layer are distinct concepts, they are often used interchangeably in practice. However, a more accurate understanding of their differences and how they work together can help advance blockchain technology's development and implementation.

2.2. *Cross-chain technologies*

According to the research conducted by Lee (2020), the key cross-chain technologies can be broadly classified into four categories.

Table 1. Pros and cons of notary schemes.

Pros	Cons
Increased liquidity: By allowing assets and data to move freely between different blockchains, cross-chain notary schemes can increase the liquidity of assets and reduce the risk of illiquidity in any single network.	*Complexity*: Cross-chain notary schemes can be complex and difficult to implement, requiring a deep understanding of both the technical and regulatory aspects of different blockchain networks.
Decentralized validation: Cross-chain notary schemes are often based on consensus algorithms, which allow for decentralized validation of transactions across different blockchain networks.	*Scalability*: Cross-chain notary schemes may face scalability challenges, as they require a large amount of computational power and network bandwidth to validate transactions across multiple networks.
	Regulation: The regulatory environment for cross-chain notary schemes is still in its early stages, and there may be regulatory hurdles that need to be overcome before these technologies can be widely adopted.
	Centralization: In some cases, cross-chain notary schemes can lead to centralization, as a small group of trusted entities may be responsible for validating transactions across different networks.

2.2.1. *Notary schemes*

In this approach, a trusted third-party entity or group is utilized to verify and declare the validity of information or events that occur on different blockchains. This mechanism acts as a notary, providing a trusted source of information between two blockchains. The advantages and disadvantages of notary schemes are discussed in Table 1.

2.2.2. *Side chains/relays*

A side chain protocol involves a mutual agreement between two blockchains to establish a two-way peg. This enables users to transfer digital assets between the main chain and the side chain, creating a seamless and secure connection between the two chains. Projects such as Cosmos and Polkadot have implemented side chain protocols in their technology. The advantages and disadvantages of side chains/relays are tabulated in Table 2.

Table 2. Pros and cons of side chains/relays.

Pros	Cons
Scalability: Side chains and relays can help to increase the scalability of a blockchain network by offloading some of its processing load to the side chain or relay.	*Complexity*: Cross-chain side chains and relays can be complex to implement and require a deep understanding of both the underlying technology and the specific use case.
Flexibility: Cross-chain side chains and relays allow for the creation of custom solutions tailored to specific use cases, enabling greater flexibility in the deployment of blockchain technology.	*Compatibility*: Side chains and relays must be compatible with both the originating blockchain network and the target network, which can limit their ability to be adopted in certain situations.
Security: Side chains and relays can enhance the security of a blockchain network by allowing for the segregation of assets and sensitive information onto separate chains, reducing the risk of a single point of failure.	*Integration*: Cross-chain side chains and relays must be integrated with existing systems, which can be challenging and require significant technical expertise.
	Trust: Cross-chain side chains and relays rely on trust between different blockchain networks, which can be difficult to establish and maintain in some situations.

2.2.3. *Hash locking*

Hash locking involves the utilization of a trigger mechanism, such as a hash of a random number, to initiate cross-chain interactions. The concept of hash locking originated from Bitcoin's Lightning Network[1] and uses Revocable Sequence Maturity Contract (RSMC) and Hash Time Locked Contract (HTLC) technologies.[2] However, its application is limited to cross-chain asset swap and does not support the transfer of cross-chain assets or the execution of cross-chain contracts. The advantages and disadvantages of hash locking are presented in Table 3.

---

[1] Bitcoin's Lightning Network is a second-layer payment protocol that operates on top of the Bitcoin blockchain. It is designed to enable faster and cheaper transactions on the Bitcoin network by moving some transactions off the main blockchain and onto the Lightning Network.

The Lightning Network creates a network of payment channels between users, allowing them to transact with each other directly without having to wait for confirmation on the main Bitcoin blockchain. This significantly reduces the time and fees associated with traditional Bitcoin transactions.

In simpler terms, Bitcoin's Lightning Network is like a shortcut for making small and quick payments using Bitcoin, without having to wait for confirmation on the main Bitcoin blockchain every time.

[2] RSMC and HTLC are two types of smart contracts used in Bitcoin's Lightning Network to facilitate secure and reliable payments.

Table 3. Pros and cons of hash locking.

Pros	Cons
Increased security: Cross-chain hash locking allows for the creation of secure and decentralized cross-chain transactions by utilizing the security of multiple blockchains.	*Complexity*: Cross-chain hash locking technology can be complex and difficult to implement, which may deter some developers from using it.
Decentralization: Cross-chain hash locking technology can help to further decentralize the cryptocurrency ecosystem by allowing for greater interaction between different blockchains.	*Limited compatibility*: Cross-chain hash locking is currently only compatible with a limited number of blockchains, which limits its overall usefulness.
	Lack of standardization: There is currently a lack of standardization in cross-chain hash locking technology, which can lead to confusion and fragmentation in the ecosystem.
	Centralization risks: Cross-chain hash locking technology may be vulnerable to centralization risks, as the use of centralized intermediaries such as Oracles can undermine its decentralization.

2.2.4. *Distributed private key control*

This method involves the use of a distributed private key generation and control technology to create a locked account on the original chain and map the corresponding assets to a different blockchain. This approach enables the transfer of assets across different blockchains in a secure and decentralized manner. An example of distributed private key control's application is the Fusion Distributed Control Rights Management (DCRM), the tech powering Chainge Finance.

RSMC is a type of smart contract that can be revoked by the sender if the payment conditions are not met within a specified time frame. This ensures that if a payment does not go as planned, the funds can be returned to the sender.

HTLC, on the other hand, is a smart contract that requires the recipient to provide a cryptographic proof of payment within a specified time frame, in order to claim the funds. If the recipient fails to provide this proof, the funds will be returned to the sender.

In simpler terms, both RSMC and HTLC are smart contracts that help ensure the security and reliability of payments made through Bitcoin's Lightning Network by setting conditions for the release of funds and providing a mechanism for the return of funds if the conditions are not met.

Table 4. Pros and cons of distributed private key control.

Pros	Cons
Security: The key is stored in multiple pieces, making it less vulnerable to theft or loss.	*Complexity*: The system is more complex than traditional private key management, making it more difficult to implement and use.
Decentralization: Multiple parties hold the key, increasing the decentralization of the system and reducing the risk of centralization.	*Limited decentralization*: Until enough parties hold the key, decentralization is not in its ideal form.
Increased trust: The key is controlled by multiple parties, reducing the risk of a single point of failure and increasing trust in the system.	

The advantages and disadvantages of distributed private key control are shown in Table 4.

The cross-chain technologies discussed above can be split into two categories:

Zero knowledge proof: It is used to pass information across chains (e.g. LayerZero). It can revolve around its reliance on existing consensus on different chains to ensure security, transparency, and a decent level of decentralization. However, its cons are directly related to the need of the targeting chains to support the virtual machine. If a specific chain does not support it, then deployment is impossible, which means limited compatibility.

Smart contracts: Using smart contracts to manage cross-chain operations (e.g. Wormhole). One of the most significant pros related to smart contracts is ease of implementation. However, compatibility is yet again an unsurpassable con as not every chain supports the smart contract feature. Furthermore, smart contracts' code has logic, which makes this tech extremely susceptible to hacks (around 80% of cross-chain related hacks are of this nature) as it will inevitably have loopholes/vulnerabilities that can be exploited. Proper auditing is near-impossible due to the extreme time-consuming nature of the task.

To conclude, the two categories aforementioned have a main common downside: limitations in compatibility. Only a limited number of chains can be interconnected by using zero knowledge proof or smart contracts.

Distributed private key control applied in the form of Fusion DCRM [Multi-party Computation (MPC) + Threshold Signature Schemes (TSS)] can ensure both compatibilities which support 99.9% of chains and security guaranteed by the multi-signature system.

DCRM does have its own shortcomings, as it's not built on the existing consensus, and a new consensus layer implies a lower degree of decentralization because of the initially low number of nodes. However, lots of chains have a limited number of nodes that can validate blocks, so this is not uncommon. DCRM is steadily increasing the number of nodes which ensures in the long run an optimal degree of decentralization.

2.3. *Classification of cross-chain*

We divide cross-chain into narrow sense and broad sense.

2.3.1. *Cross-chain in the narrow sense*

2.3.1.1. Token exchange among different chains

Before the invention of cross-chain bridges, users could only exchange tokens of different chains through centralized exchanges. For example, suppose Alice wants to exchange BTC into ETH. In that case, she needs to deposit BTC to a centralized exchange, trade it into ETH, and then withdraw it to Ethereum.

With the atomic exchange technology of Hash Time Locked Contract, Alice can directly exchange BTC into ETH on the chain. Atomic exchange is a technology that facilitates secure and reliable cryptocurrency trades between different blockchain networks without needing a trusted third party. The term "atomic" refers to the exchange being either completed or canceled, and the assets involved are returned to original owners if canceled.

An atomic exchange works by using smart contracts to lock up the traded assets and automatically release them when certain conditions are met, such as the successful completion of the trade or the passage of a specified period. If the conditions are not met, the assets are automatically returned to their original owners.

In simpler terms, atomic exchange is a way for people to trade cryptocurrencies between different blockchain networks securely and reliably, without needing a trusted third party. The exchange is either completed successfully or canceled, with the assets involved being returned to their original owners.

2.3.1.2. Token transfer among different chains

Blockchains are isolated, so a chain cannot transfer tokens directly to another chain. With the cross-chain bridge technology, users can lock the original tokens in the source chain and mint the same amount of wrapped tokens in the destination chain to transfer tokens. A typical example is the wrapped BTC on Ethereum.

A cross-chain bridge is a technology that enables communication and transfer of assets between different blockchain networks. Essentially, it acts as a link between two different blockchains, allowing for the exchange of digital assets, information, and even smart contracts between the two networks.

The purpose of a cross-chain bridge is to enable interoperability between different blockchain networks, breaking down the barriers between isolated blockchain ecosystems and enabling a more connected and seamless crypto-world. With cross-chain bridges, users can move their assets between different blockchains, access decentralized applications on other networks, and take advantage of the unique features of each blockchain ecosystem.

2.3.2. *Cross-chain in the broad sense*

2.3.2.1. Message transmission among different chains

The message here refers to any cross-chain requests by users, including token exchange and transfer.

The cross-chain is messaging between blockchains. Blockchain *A* can read the status and requests of blockchain *B* by messaging. It is the trigger condition for execution. For example, a token transfer is completed by two cross-chain messages. The first is to pass the message of blockchain *A* to blockchain *B*. After verifying the message's authenticity, blockchain *B* mints the wrapped tokens and feeds back this state to blockchain *A*.

Using the cross-chain message transmission protocol, developers can make many cross-chain dApps, such as cross-chain bridge, cross-chain lending, cross-chain NFT, cross-chain aggregation, cross-chain derivatives, etc.

A cross-chain message transmission protocol is a set of rules and standards that enable communication and the exchange of messages between different blockchain networks. It provides common language and framework for different blockchains to communicate and interact with each other, enabling interoperability and breaking down the barriers between isolated blockchain ecosystems.

The purpose of a cross-chain message transmission protocol is to allow blockchains to exchange data and information, such as transaction data, in a secure and reliable manner. This enables users to move assets between different blockchains, access decentralized applications on other networks, and take advantage of the unique features of each blockchain ecosystem.

3. Important Cross-chain Message Transmission Protocols

In the above section, we learned that the essence of cross-chain is messaging between blockchains. This section will introduce how several cross-chain messaging protocols work.

3.1. *The IBC protocol*

If we say that Ethereum is a supercomputer, Cosmos is a blockchain Internet that connects independent servers into a network. Cosmos is not a blockchain but an underlying protocol for designing an application-specific blockchain (called zone).

The key components of the Cosmos network are as follows: According to Tendermint, Inc. (2022), Cosmos is a blockchain Internet that connects independent servers into a network, offering an underlying protocol for designing application-specific blockchains, known as zones. The Cosmos ecosystem consists of the Tendermint consensus protocol, Cosmos SDK, and Inter-Blockchain Communication protocol. The Cosmos SDK provides basic functional modules such as staking, governance, and IBC, reducing the development costs and allowing developers to focus on building application-specific solutions. The IBC protocol enables communication and interoperability between zones, providing shared security to all blockchains in the Cosmos network. Cosmos provides a comprehensive solution for building and deploying scalable, interoperable, and secure blockchain applications. The network's modular design and flexible architecture allow developers to create custom blockchain solutions tailored to their specific needs and use cases. Please see the structure of Cosmos hub and zone at Fig. 1.

For a blockchain to be compatible with IBC, it must have instant finality, meaning transactions must be processed quickly and without the possibility of tampering. Blockchains that use Proof of Work (PoW), such as Bitcoin and Ethereum, use a peg-zone[3] instead of IBC to communicate with the Cosmos network.

[3]A peg-zone is a special type of blockchain that acts as a bridge between blockchains that use Proof of Work consensus mechanisms and the Cosmos network. The Cosmos network uses the Tendermint consensus protocol, which is a Byzantine Fault Tolerance consensus engine that provides instant finality for transactions.

Because Bitcoin and Ethereum, for example, use PoW consensus, they cannot directly communicate with the Cosmos network through the IBC protocol. To overcome this, a peg-zone is used to link these PoW blockchains to the Cosmos network.

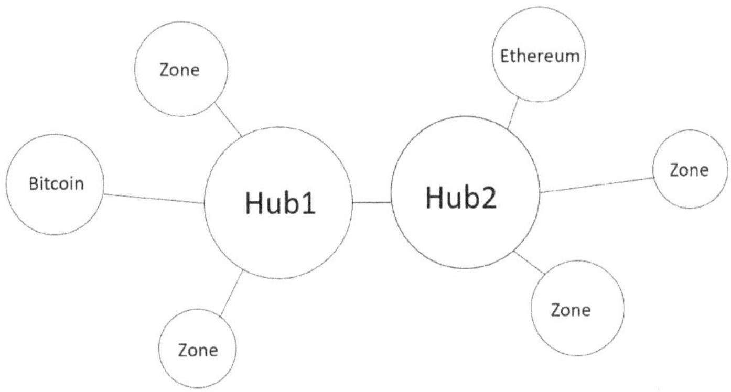

Fig. 1. Structure of Cosmos hub and zone.

The IBC protocol works as follows: Lightweight clients run on each blockchain and receive block headers from other blockchains. This allows each blockchain to keep track of the validators on other blockchains. When blockchain *A* wants to transfer tokens to blockchain *B*, it must first stake tokens on blockchain *A* and send the proof of stake to blockchain *B*. Blockchain *B* then verifies the proof using the block header from blockchain *A*. Upon confirmation, blockchain *B* will issue wrapped tokens. The same process is used for withdrawing tokens back to blockchain *A*.

3.2. *LayerZero*

LayerZero is an omnichain interoperability protocol, which is different from the generic term Layer 0. Layer 0 refers to the underlying infrastructure or foundational layer of a technology stack. In the context of blockchain, Layer 0 refers to the "base layer" or fundamental building blocks that make up a blockchain system, such as the consensus mechanism, networking protocols, and cryptographic algorithms. LayerZero, on the other hand, is a protocol that enables multiple blockchain networks to interact and exchange information with each other, allowing for

---

The peg-zone serves as a trustless intermediary, allowing assets to be transferred between PoW blockchains and the Cosmos network. When a user wants to transfer assets from a PoW blockchain to the Cosmos network, they first deposit the assets into the peg-zone. The peg-zone then issues wrapped tokens that can be transferred over the IBC protocol to the Cosmos network. When the user wants to withdraw the assets back to the PoW blockchain, they simply unwrap the tokens and withdraw the original assets.

In this way, the peg-zone enables communication and interoperability between PoW blockchains and the Cosmos network, despite their differing consensus mechanisms.

seamless communication and transfer of assets between different blockchain platforms.

According to Zarick (2021b), LayerZero aims to address the challenges faced by the middle chain and the IBC protocol.

The middle chain, which has full signing authority for all messaging, poses a significant risk of hacking. While this approach offers a relatively low cost for cross-chain transactions, it is not secure.

On the other hand, connecting Ethereum and other EVM-based blockchains through the Cosmos IBC is more secure but comes with a higher cost. Additionally, the IBC transport layer only allows direct communication between blockchains that have instant finality.

LayerZero is an omnichain interoperability protocol that offers a cost-effective and faster alternative to these existing solutions. It ensures security through the use of Oracles and Relayers, making it a secure and efficient solution for cross-chain transactions.

How does LayerZero achieve this vision?

LayerZero introduces the concept of ultra-light nodes (ULNs), which offer cost-effective security solutions. ULN performs the same validation as an on-chain light node and provides the same level of security. Instead of storing all block headers sequentially, block headers are streamed on demand by decentralized oracles.[4]

When a dApp wants to send a message from blockchain *A* to blockchain *B*, it sends the message through the LayerZero Endpoint of blockchain *A*.[5] The message is then notified to the Oracle and Relayer, which forward the block header to the

---

[4] Block headers are a crucial part of the blockchain that store information about each block in the chain. The process of "streaming on demand" means that these block headers are not stored in a sequential manner like in traditional light nodes, but are instead requested and delivered as needed.

In the context of LayerZero, block headers are streamed on demand by decentralized Oracles. This means that when a dApp wants to send a message from one blockchain to another, it sends a request for the necessary block headers to the decentralized Oracle. The Oracle then retrieves and forwards the requested block headers to the LayerZero Endpoint, allowing for the successful transfer of the message from one blockchain to another.

The use of decentralized Oracles to stream block headers on demand offers a cost-effective solution for cross-chain transactions, as it eliminates the need for light nodes to store all block headers sequentially.

[5] In the context of LayerZero, a "LayerZero Endpoint" refers to a gateway or a connection point between two different blockchains. It acts as a bridge between two different blockchains, allowing for the seamless transfer of information and assets between them.

The LayerZero Endpoint acts as an intermediary between the dApps sending the message and the target blockchain receiving the message. When a dApp wants to send a message from one blockchain to another, it sends the message through the LayerZero Endpoint of the originating blockchain.

LayerZero Endpoint of blockchain *B*. The Relayer submits the transaction proof, and after the block header and proof have been verified, the message is forwarded to the destination address.

In this way, LayerZero provides a secure and efficient solution for cross-chain transactions through ultra-light nodes and decentralized Oracles and Relayers.

Adding an independent Relayer to the existing Oracle increases safety. The Relayer can enable blockchain *B* to verify what happened to the blockchain again. It is not easy to beat Chainlink[6] DONs (Decentralized Oracle Networks),[7] which are the default Oracle in the example illustrated in Fig. 2. Even if the Oracle is

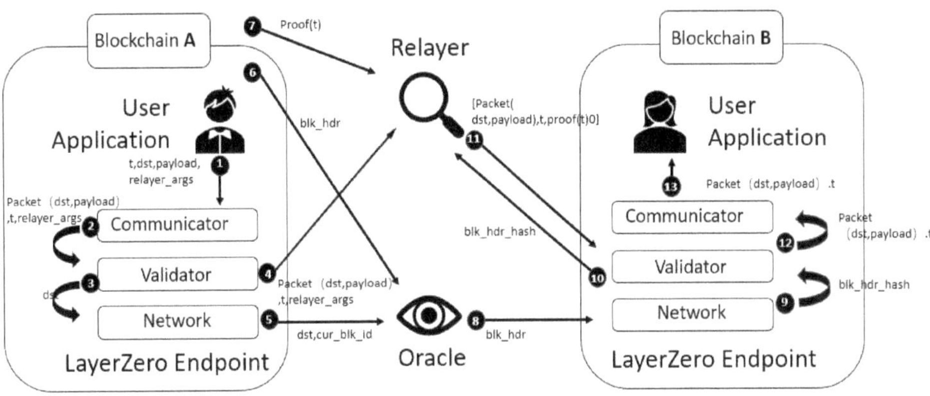

Fig. 2. Message transmission process of LayerZero.

The endpoint then forwards the message to the target blockchain, ensuring that the message is delivered to its intended recipient.

In this way, the LayerZero Endpoint acts as a crucial component of the LayerZero protocol, allowing for cross-chain transactions to occur in a secure and efficient manner.

[6] Chainlink (LINK) is a decentralized Oracle network that provides reliable data to smart contracts on the blockchain. It enables smart contracts to access off-chain data and events, such as financial data, weather data, or even data from IoT devices, in a secure and decentralized manner.

Chainlink Oracles work by providing real-world data to smart contracts, and in doing so, they increase the capabilities and utility of smart contracts by enabling them to interact with real-world data and events. This opens up a wide range of possibilities for the development of new decentralized applications and use cases for blockchain technology.

The Chainlink (LINK) DON is powered by the Ethereum token called LINK. This network enables Ethereum smart contracts to connect to other data sources, payment systems, and application user interfaces securely. Chainlink tokens (LINKs) are used as a form of payment for Oracle services within the network, incentivizing node operators to provide accurate and reliable data to the network. The token economics of Chainlink also ensures that there is a robust and decentralized network of Oracles available to service the needs of the smart contracts on the network.

[7] See the whitepaper "Chainlink 2.0 and the future of Decentralized Oracle Networks" for more details at: https://chain.link/whitepaper.

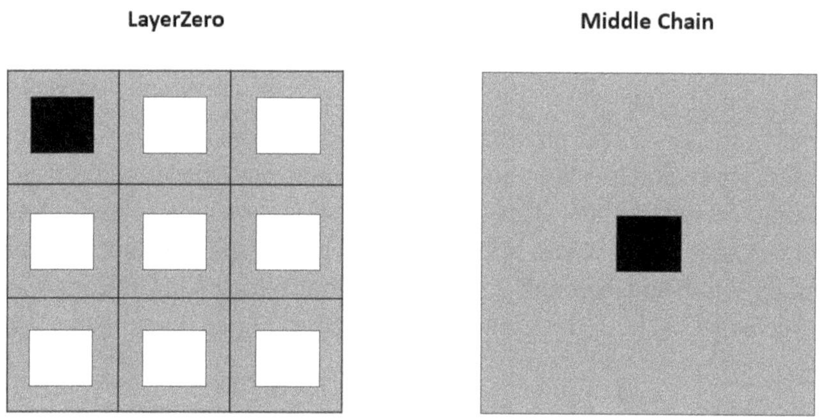

Fig. 3. LayerZero versus middle chains.

broken, there is Relayer verification. The worst case is that Oracle *A* and Relayer *A* collude. All risks are borne by the dApps receiving the message from Oracle *A* and Relayer *A*. Those dApps using other Relayers or Oracles will not be affected. Fig. 3. shows the advantage of LayerZero when encountering attack. For the middle chain solution, the whole system would crash if a single point is attacked. The dApps based on LayerZero can choose their trusted Oracle, and even establish their Relayer. These double or multiple verification methods ensure more confirmation points than a single point.

3.3. *Celer Inter-chain Message framework*

Celer Inter-chain Message (Celer IM) is a cross-chain infrastructure designed for developers. It allows them to easily turn their independently deployed dApps into native cross-chain applications by using a simple contract plugin. This eliminates the need for complex procedures and enables users to access cross-chain functionality while staying on a single chain.

The Celer IM architecture consists of two main components (Celer Network, 2022a). The first is the message bus smart contract, which acts as a "mailbox" on the chain. The second is the State Guardian Network (SGN), which serves as the "messenger" connecting various blockchains and facilitating the transmission of messages. SGN is a proof-of-stake chain based on the Cosmos

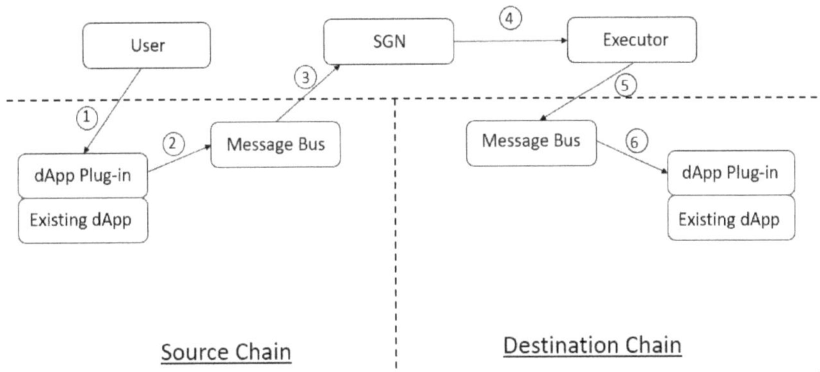

Fig. 4. Message transmission process of Celer IM.

Tendermint consensus, and validators must stake CELR tokens[8] to participate in this network.

Instead of directly interacting with the existing dApp's smart contract, users interact with the new dApp plugin contract (as shown in Fig. 4) to initiate cross-chain requests. This is the only interaction between users and the cross-chain dApp. The dApp plugin, a part of the dApp, then sends the user's cross-chain request as a message to the message bus smart contract on the source chain (Step 2). The SGN monitors the message bus smart contract, and all validators verify the message's existence and generate a weighted multi-sign proof. The proof is stored on the SGN chain, waiting for the Executor to relay it to the message bus on the destination chain (Steps 4 and 5). The message bus smart contract on the destination chain verifies the message's validity and delivers it to the dApp in the destination chain. The recipient in the destination chain executes the corresponding tasks according to the message.

The security of Celer IM depends on SGN. The security model provided by SGN is similar to other Layer-1 blockchains based on Tendermint. As long as a node is malicious, it will be slashed by the cross-chain consensus protocol. This mechanism has been verified countless times in practice.

[8]CELR token is the native cryptocurrency of the Celer Network, a Layer-2 scaling solution for blockchain applications.

What if most validators are malicious? The possibility is relatively low. Celer IM also uses the second safety model similar to the Optimistic Rollup,[9] to prevent black swans in extreme cases. When a cross-chain message arrives at the destination chain through SGN, the message will not be immediately sent to the relevant application to execute the corresponding requests. However, it will be isolated for some time. During isolation, the application developer and the operator of each SGN node can go to the source chain for verification. This mode uses additional isolation delay to obtain a more robust trust-any security model. The system is still safe as long as one of the SGN nodes keeps running. In practical application, cBridge developed by Celer Network, combines two security models. For small transfers, it depends on SGN to execute immediately. For large transfers, it is executed through the isolation period.

The above are three crucial cross-chain messaging protocols. We mentioned that the essence of cross-chain is a combination of messaging. Next, let us dive into the cross-chain solutions of assets, which are the most frequent cross-chain requests.

4. Cross-chain Solutions for Tokens

4.1. *Centralized exchange*

A Centralized Exchange is a secure platform for cross-chain transactions. There are no worries about transactions not being completed. However, it comes with some drawbacks, such as centralized custody, privacy concerns, limited chain support, and complicated operation.

---

[9] Optimistic Rollup is a Layer-2 scaling solution for blockchain networks that allows for faster and cheaper transactions while maintaining the security guarantees of the underlying network. It works by aggregating multiple transactions into a single transaction that is then executed on the main blockchain. The result of this single transaction is then stored on the main blockchain, allowing for a significantly increased transaction throughput compared to executing each transaction individually. The key innovation of Optimistic Rollup is the use of fraud proofs, which allow for the detection and reversal of any malicious transactions that may occur within the Rollup. A fraud proof is a mechanism used in the context of blockchain technology to prove that a specific event or transaction has occurred fraudulently. It is essentially a proof that a party has acted in a malicious or dishonest manner and has violated the rules and expectations of the network. Fraud proofs can be used to challenge transactions, blocks, or other events on a blockchain, allowing the network to identify and reject fraudulent activities. This helps to maintain the integrity and security of the blockchain and to prevent malicious actors from compromising the system.

In some cases, fraud proofs may be based on zero-knowledge proofs, which allow nodes to prove the validity of a transaction or block without revealing the underlying data. In other cases, fraud proofs may be based on more traditional cryptographic techniques, such as digital signatures or hash functions.

4.2. *Official cross-chain bridge*

Many blockchains have launched their official cross-chain bridges, such as Avalanche-Ethereum Bridge (AEB),[10] Wormhole of Solana,[11] and Rainbow Bridge of Near.[12] These bridges aim to bring assets into their blockchain ecosystems. However, they come at a higher cost than third-party cross-chain bridges, and their usage can be less convenient. For instance, it takes seven days to transfer assets from Arbitrum to Ethereum using the official bridge.

4.3. *Asset-specific bridge*

An asset-specific bridge is a technology that enables the transfer of a specific asset, such as a token, between two different blockchain networks. This type of bridge is designed only to support the transfer of a specific asset, rather than providing a general solution for cross-chain transfers. The purpose of an asset-specific bridge is to increase interoperability and provide users with a secure and decentralized method of moving a specific asset between different blockchain networks. The use of asset-specific bridges can help to improve the accessibility and liquidity of certain assets within the broader blockchain ecosystem.

Cross-chain bridges, like BitGo, Ren Protocol, Keep Network, and others, can transfer non-smart contract-compatible native tokens (e.g. BTC, Dogecoin, and Zcash) to blockchains with smart contract functionality, allowing users to benefit from DeFi. However, these bridges come with the risk of centralized management.

---

[10] Avalanche Ethereum Bridge is a technology that allows for the transfer of assets, such as tokens, between the Avalanche network and the Ethereum network. The bridge enables users to take advantage of the features and benefits of both networks while also providing a seamless, secure, and decentralized method of moving assets between the two. The bridge is intended to enhance interoperability and provide a link between Ethereum and Avalanche, rendering users with greater flexibility and accessibility to the benefits of each network.

[11] Wormhole of Solana is a platform that enables the transfer of assets between the Solana blockchain and other blockchain networks. The Wormhole provides a bridge between Solana and other blockchains, allowing users to move assets such as tokens and cryptocurrencies between the two networks in a secure and decentralized manner. The goal of the Wormhole is to enhance interoperability and provide greater flexibility for users by allowing them to take advantage of the unique features and benefits of both Solana and other blockchains. This allows users to access a wider range of assets and opportunities in the broader blockchain ecosystem.

[12] Rainbow Bridge of Near is a technology that enables the transfer of assets, such as tokens, between the Near blockchain and other blockchain networks.

4.4. *The third-party cross-chain bridge*

A third-party cross-chain bridge is a technology that enables the transfer of assets, such as tokens, between different blockchain networks. This type of bridge is provided by a third-party entity, rather than the blockchain networks. It is designed to provide a secure and decentralized solution for cross-chain transfers. The purpose of a third-party cross-chain bridge is to increase interoperability and provide users with greater flexibility by allowing them to access the unique features and benefits of multiple blockchain networks.

Third-party cross-chain bridges offer efficient cross-chain services at a low cost. They support many tokens across multiple blockchains, but the level of security they provide varies widely. Leading projects in this field include Celer Network, Multichain, and Synapse protocol.

4.5. *The cross-chain bridge aggregator*

A cross-chain bridge aggregator acts as a hub for multiple cross-chain bridges, allowing users to access multiple blockchains from a single entry point. The purpose of a cross-chain bridge aggregator is to increase accessibility and convenience for users by allowing them to perform cross-chain transfers more efficiently. The aggregator acts as a layer between the user and the different blockchains, allowing for the consolidation of multiple cross-chain bridges into a single platform. The use of a cross-chain bridge aggregator can help to simplify the process of performing cross-chain transfers and reduce the barriers to entry for users within the broader blockchain ecosystem.

The aggregator collects information about the different bridges available, including their fees, security measures, speed, and compatibility with different assets, and uses this information to provide recommendations to users. By aggregating the mainstream cross-chain bridges, the aggregator helps users to find the best bridge for their needs, depending on the assets they wish to transfer, the speed they require, and the security they prefer. This can significantly simplify the process of performing cross-chain transactions, reducing the need for users to research and compare multiple bridges on their own. In this way, the cross-chain bridge aggregator plays an important role in increasing accessibility and convenience for users within the broader blockchain ecosystem.

5. Types of Cross-chain Bridges

Cardfarm (2021) outlined three common constructions for how cross-chain bridges work: (1) Lock and Mint, (2) Atomic Swaps, and (3) Liquidity Providers (LPs). These are different approaches to building a cross-chain bridge. Each of these constructions has its strengths and weaknesses, and the choice of construction will depend on the specific needs and requirements of the user. The details of each construction can be explored further to gain a deeper understanding of the different approaches to cross-chain bridges.

5.1. *Lock and mint*

This cross-chain bridge method involves the transfer of tokens between two blockchains by locking the tokens on the source chain and minting the corresponding wrapped tokens on the destination chain. The process of token transfer involves the following steps:

1. The user sends the tokens to the smart contract of the cross-chain bridge on the source chain and provides their receiving address on the destination chain.
2. The validator nodes on the destination chain verify this information and the bridge mints the wrapped tokens at the user's specified receiving address.
3. To return the tokens to the source chain, the user sends the wrapped tokens to the smart contract of the cross-chain bridge on the destination chain and specifies their wallet address.
4. The validators on the destination chain then burn the wrapped tokens, unlock the tokens on the source chain, and transfer them to the user's wallet address.

The security of this method is dependent on the validators, and any malicious behavior or hacking of the validators can result in significant economic loss.

5.2. *Atomic Swaps based on Hashed Time Locked Contract*

HTLC is a smart contract mechanism utilized in blockchain applications to minimize counterparty risk. The process works as follows using the example of swapping 1 BTC for 10 ETH:

1. User A generates a random private key R, calculates its hash value, m = hash(R), and sends m to user B. At the same time, they initiate a transaction to transfer 1 BTC to user B, with the condition that user B must present the private key R within the specified time frame for the transaction to be successful.
2. Upon receiving the transaction initiated by user A, user B transfers 10 ETH to user A with the condition that user A must present R within the specified time frame for the transaction to succeed.
3. After receiving the transaction initiated by user B, user A reveals the value of R, which makes the transaction initiated by B successful and allows user B to receive 10 ETH. The value of R is then disclosed to user B.

In step 3, user B obtains the value of R from user A, which allows the transaction initiated by A to succeed, and user B receives 1 BTC.

However, this method has several disadvantages, such as the following:

1. The absence of a peer-to-peer counterparty may result in waiting time.
2. The mechanism's complexity leads to high transaction fees.
3. Counterparties have the discretion to complete the transaction based on the real-time swap rate, making it unsuitable for large transactions.
4. Token transfer cannot be realized through this approach.

5.3. *Liquidity providers*

A cross-chain bridge that deploys smart contracts on multiple blockchains enables users to provide liquidity, thereby improving cross-chain efficiency and reducing capital costs. The decentralized validator nodes and efficient transfer ensure adequate liquidity.

Such cross-chain bridges will encourage users to provide liquidity and allocate funds according to needs. This eliminates the issue of fragmented liquidity caused by atomic exchange methods. However, the potential risks include the possibility of the cross-chain bridge losing control over tokens and potential bugs in the smart contracts.

6. The Bridging Trilemma

The Bridging Trilemma, as described by Zarick (2021a), states that when designing bridges between multiple blockchain networks, designers must make a tradeoff between three key features. These features are as follows:

Instant Guaranteed Finality. This refers to the assurance that funds will be immediately available on the destination chain once a transaction is successfully committed on the source chain.
Unified Liquidity. This refers to the ability of users to access a single pool of liquidity across multiple chains.
Native Assets. These refer to the availability of the user's preferred assets (either native or highly liquid synthetic assets) on the destination chain.

The Trilemma posits that designers can only choose one or two of these features, and must sacrifice the others. This highlights the challenge of creating bridges that balance the needs of users and the limitations of the technology.

7. Leading Third-party Cross-chain Bridge

The third-party cross-chain bridge is the subdivision that received the most funding in the cross-chain solution. It is also the tool most used by users. Hop Protocol, Across Protocol, deBridge, Multichain, and many other protocols are active players in this field. Each of these cross-chain bridges offers its own set of features and solutions to the challenges faced in the field of cross-chain transactions. However, all three share the goal of providing users with a seamless, secure, and efficient cross-chain experience. Let us see how three well-known bridges work.

7.1. *Gravity bridge*

BNB had been the only token that existed simultaneously on Ethereum and the Cosmos ecosystem for a long time. Until the opening of the Gravity Bridge, applications within the Cosmos ecosystem were not accessible to Ethereum users. The Gravity Bridge serves as a neutral link that connects Ethereum with blockchains based on the Cosmos SDK, allowing the Cosmos ecosystem to communicate with the proof-of-work chain for the first time.

According to Tremback (2021), the Gravity Bridge enables users to transfer tokens from Ethereum to Cosmos and vice versa by locking and minting. The Gravity Bridge can also be used on any blockchain within the Cosmos ecosystem, including Cosmos Hub, Osmosis, and Stargaze. Tokens such as WBTC, WETH, and WUSDC can be utilized on Cosmos dApps, such as Akash Network, Sentinel, Regen, and Osmosis. Additionally, Cosmos ecosystem tokens, like ATOM, can also be transferred to Ethereum for DeFi mining.

The forfeiture mechanism guarantees that validators will only sign or transmit messages if there is consensus within the Cosmos ecosystem. The ecosystem is home to numerous active validators who must stake valuable collateral to participate.

If any validator engages in malicious behavior, they risk facing financial penalties with the slashing of the tokens. Anyone can submit proof to slash malicious validators. Validators are permissionless and censorship-resistant. Each validator verifies every deposit that occurred in Ethereum to ensure security.

7.2. *Stargate*

Stargate is the first protocol based on LayerZero, enabling users to transfer and exchange native tokens between blockchains quickly.

Stargate promises to deliver a low-cost and seamless user experience, unlike many existing cross-chain bridges that rely on wrapped tokens. Most of the cross-chain bridges are still wrapped tokens. The transaction cost is high, and the long cross-chain process results in a poor user experience.

The Trilemma problem, a major challenge faced by cross-chain solutions, is effectively addressed by Stargate. By leveraging LayerZero, Stargate overcomes the limitations faced by traditional cross-chain bridges and provides a unique solution to the cross-chain conundrum.

LayerZero helps Stargate achieve instant guaranteed finality. According to Zarick *et al.* (2021), Stargate uses its delta algorithm to provide unified liquidity and transfer of native tokens. For the same token, all chains use a unified liquidity pool, and each chain can access the liquidity of other chains. The Delta algorithm is a balancing algorithm that supports the native token pool. It manages liquidity with a "soft-partitioned" method to prevent multiple simultaneous requests from running on the liquidity pool. For example, in a network consisting of *X*-, *Y*-, and *Z*-chains, the $100 liquidity available on the *X*-chain is simulated into $50 on the *Y*-chain and $50 on the *Z*-chain. Delta algorithm monitors the "virtual balance sheet" of each chain. The protocol allows "borrowing" and "repaying" liquidity between different chains, thus allowing the algorithm to maintain a liquidity balance in the face of unbalanced transaction volumes. However, when the divisional balance drops below the initial value, a "debt" appears. When a transfer request from source chain *A* to destination chain *B* occurs, the tokens deposited in source chain *A* will first repay the "debt" on chain *A*, and the remaining funds will be distributed among all pools according to the weight.

Stargate is a project that received funds from FTX, a16z, Sequoia, Binance, Coinbase, and many other leading investment companies. There are nearly 4 billion Total Values Locked (TVLs) after being launched within 10 days, ranking 11th among all protocols (ranked 27th on August 7 with 491.15m TVLs).

7.3. *cBridge 2.0*

According to Celer Network (2021a), cBridge 2.0 is blockchain interoperability powered by the State Guardian Network.

SGN is a POS chain based on Tendermint, which monitors events on the chain. In cBridge 2.0, decentralized SGN manages to share a liquidity pool on multiple chains. Liquidity Providers provide liquidity to SGN to receive fees without running the nodes themselves.

Is it safe to use SGN as the shared liquidity pool manager? First of all, SGN adopts the PoS consensus. The liquidity pool may be at risk only when more than two-thirds of the nodes are malicious. The cost of malicious nodes will increase along with the value of cBridge Network. SGN is safer than multi-signature and private key distribution solutions because they do not require token staking. Their security cannot grow with the network value. There is a potential risk of collusion between multi-signature validators or private key holders in the face of substantial economic benefits. SGN allows new validators to be elected and join the validator set through the staking governance. However, the price of staking tokens may fall seriously when the market goes down. The staking value may be far lower than the liquidity on the cross-chain bridge. Users and the team should be vigilant against the potential risks committed by the validators.

Some cross-chain bridges require Liquidity Providers to put token liquidity into the AMM pool, such as Thorchain and Hop Protocol. Under this model, Liquidity Providers face additional costs when adding, removing, and rebalancing liquidity across multiple chains. Thorchain requires LP to use the RUNE token whose price is not stable. Thus, the Liquidity Provider risks impermanent loss. Hop Protocol needs bonders to provide liquidity, and the efficiency is low because the actual demand for liquidity of cross-chain transfer is twice the need of users.

When cBridge 2.0 processes cross-chain requests, SGN uses the liquidity of the whole pool to calculate the slippage and pricing. Then SGN regards LP as a "virtual cBridge node" and allocates cross-chain requests according to the liquidity of LP. The liquidity balance of the destination chain will decrease in proportion to its available liquidity, while the liquidity balance on the source chain will increase. In addition, cBridge 2.0 also uses random sampling and approximation algorithms to minimize costs and maintain statistical fairness between Liquidity Providers. This design allows each Liquidity Provider to see how their liquidity is allocated at any given time. It will enable them to fully understand the current situation when they choose to remove or increase the liquidity of any chain.

cBridge is the default bridge of BAS, the side chain of the BNB Chain. It reflects Binance's acknowledgment of Celer Technology.

8. Other Cross-chain Applications

The cross-chain messaging protocol is not limited to use with the cross-chain bridge but can be utilized in a variety of interoperability scenarios.

8.1. *Cross-chain aggregator*

A Cross-chain Aggregator is a solution designed to help users access cross-chain transactions with lower costs and faster speeds. It achieves this by providing a unified platform for users to compare and choose the most cost-effective and fast cross-chain options available. Some popular protocols in this field include Bridge Eye, Bungee, and XY Finance. These protocols work by aggregating data from multiple chains and presenting it in a single place, making it easier for users to compare different options and make informed decisions.

8.2. *Cross-chain DeFi*

Cross-chain DeFi allows users to do DeFi strategies such as swapping, lending, and farming within a protocol by utilizing liquidities among different blockchains. Below are some examples.

- Chainhop DEX supports users in converting the ETH of Arbitrum into BNB on the BNB Chain.
- deBridge allows users to swap ETH from Ethereum to BTC on Polygon and stake the BTC at AAVE by only one request.
- Aperture Finance, the community-driven DeFi strategy, enables users of any blockchain to access the supported DeFi strategies.
- Synfutures Protocol can carry out Multi-chain Derivatives trading.
- Compound Finance allows users to deposit assets in Ethereum and borrow Dai in Polygon.

8.3. *Cross-chain DAO*

Cross-chain governance refers to decentralized decisions made by voting at the mainnet and broadcasting the result to other blockchains to execute. Here are a few examples.

- Users of AAVE vote for governance in Ethereum. Through the cross-chain governance bridge of AAVE, the bridge executor transmits the voting result to Polygon to ensure that the governance of AAVE in Ethereum can control the Polygon market of AAVE and replace the original multi-sign solution.
- FutureSwap, a decentralized transaction protocol based on AMM, completes cross-chain governance.

8.4. *Cross-chain NFT*

Cross-chain NFT means the NFT can be transferred or utilized among different chains.

- The Flow Blockchain's NBA TopShot (NFTs) can be staked at NFTfi for loans.
- The ENS domain name service is used beyond Ethereum.

9. Noteworthy Risks

Buterin (2022) expressed his optimism regarding a multi-chain blockchain ecosystem, but pessimism toward cross-chain applications. He argued that even if a 51% attacker tries to steal users' ETH, it would not succeed because such an action would violate the protocol rules and be rejected by the network. The blocks produced by the remaining 1% of the network, following the protocol rules, would be followed by everyone running a node. However, if Ethereum is attacked and controlled by 51% of its power or stake, the Solana-WETH contract would no longer be fully backed by the tokens locked on Ethereum, meaning that 1 WETH could not be exchanged for 1 ETH in its entirety.

Buterin (2022) also mentioned that when the cross-chain bridge has massive liquidity, hackers have the motivation to launch attacks to obtain substantial economic benefits. Therefore, Liquidity Providers should assess the risk when providing liquidity, and users should form the habit of canceling authorization after using the cross-chain bridge. The contract of Multichain Bridge once had bugs, and the users who did not cancel the contract in time suffered losses.

Building cross-chain bridges is a high-risk business. Chainalysis (2022) reported that $2 billion in cryptocurrency has been stolen from cross-chain bridges across 13 separate hacks this year. Attacks on cross-chain bridges account for 69% of total funds stolen by August 2, 2022. See Table 5.

Behnke (2022) summarized how cross-chain bridges are hacked into three categories:

Table 5. Several big loss events of cross-chain bridge.

Date	Cross-chain bridge	Cause of accident	Funds stolen	Status
2021.7.11	ChainSwap	Based on a report by ChainSwap (2021), there is a bug in the token cross-chain quota code. The on-chain swap bridge quota is automatically increased by the signature node, which is intended to be more decentralized without manual control. However, a logical flaw in code led to an exploit by allowing invalid addresses which weren't whitelisted to automatically increase the amount.	8 million	Issued new tokens
2021.8.10	Poly Network	Based on a report by SlowMist (2021), this attack is mainly because the keeper of the EthCrossChainData contract can be modified by the EthCrossChainManager contract, and the verifyHeaderAndExecuteTx function of the EthCrossChainManager contract can execute the data passed in by the user through the _ executeCrossChainTx function. Therefore, the attacker uses this function to pass in carefully constructed data to modify the keeper of the EthCrossChainData contract.	610 million	Hacker returned tokens
2022.1.18	Multichain	Based on the report by Beosin (2022a), the root cause was that the anySwapOutUnderlyingWithPermit function does not check the legitimacy of the token passed in by the user and does not consider that not all underlying tokens have a permit function implemented, resulting in unauthorized transfers out of the user's assets.	1.34 million	Reimbursed users' losses
2022.1.28	Qbridge	Based on a report by SlowMist (2022a), the main reason for this exploit is under the condition that the recharge of the ordinary token and that of the native token are carried out independently. When the token in the whitelist is transferred, it is not checked again	80 million	Reimbursed users' 2% losses

Table 5. (*Continued*)

Date	Cross-chain bridge	Cause of accident	Funds stolen	Status
		whether it is the zero address. This results in the operation that should have been recharged through the native recharge function to smoothly pass the ordinary token recharge function.		
2022.2.2	Wormhole	Based on a report by Wormhole (2022b), the root cause of the exploit was a bug in the signature verification code of the core Wormhole contract on Solana. This bug allowed the attacker to forge a message from the Guardians to mint Wormhole-wrapped Ether.	320 million	Reimbursed users' losses
2022.2.6	Meter Passport	Based on a report by Alo (2022), the deposit method of the ERC20 Handler contracts had the ability to automatically wrap and unwrap native gas tokens to enhance user experience. The implementation of this functionality introduced a vulnerability.	4.2 million	Issued new tokens and will use future income to buy back tokens
2022.3.29	Ronin Network	Based on a report by Ronin Network (2022), employees of Sky Mavis were under advanced spear-phishing attacks and one employee was compromised. The attacker penetrated Sky Mavis IT infrastructure and controlled the 4/9 validator nodes. The attacker found a backdoor through gas-free RPC node to get the signature for the Axie DAO validator.	620 million	Reimbursed users' losses
2022.6.24	Horizon Bridge	According to Barrett (2022), the hacker compromised at least two out of four private keys of the bridge validators.	100 million	In process
2022.8.2	Nomad Bridge	Based on a report by Nomad Bridge (2022), an implementation bug caused the Replica contract to fail to authenticate messages properly. This issue allowed any message to be forged as long as it had not already been processed. As a result, contracts relying	190 million	In process

(*Continued*)

Table 5. (*Continued*)

Date	Cross-chain bridge	Cause of accident	Funds stolen	Status
		on the Replica for authentication of inbound messages suffered security failures. This authentication failure resulted in fraudulent messages being passed to the Nomad BridgeRouter contract.		
2022.10.2	Transit Swap	Based on a report by SlowMist (2022b), the Transit Swap protocol does not strictly validate the data passed in by the user during token exchange, which results in an arbitrary external call.	23 million	Promised to cover all losses; Reimbursed 68% fund
2022.10.6	BSC Token Hub	Based on a report by Beosin (2022), BSC Token Hub uses a special pre-compiled contract for validating IAVL trees when performing cross-chain transaction verification. A bug in its implementation may allow an attacker to forge arbitrary messages.	586 million	The loss is on BNB Chain, and users were not affected.

False Deposit Events. A cross-chain bridge will monitor deposit events on one blockchain to initiate a transfer to the other. Suppose an attacker can generate a deposit event without making a real deposit or by depositing with a valueless token. In that case, they can withdraw value from the bridge at the other end. This happened in the Qubit hack, where a legacy deposit function in the code enabled fake deposits to the bridge contract.

Fake Deposits. Cross-chain bridges perform validation of a deposit before allowing a transfer to go through. If an attacker can create a fake deposit that validates as real, then they can defeat the validation process. This was the case with the Wormhole hack, where the attacker exploited a flaw in digital signature validation to steal $326 million.

Validator Takeover. Some cross-chain bridges have a set of validators that vote whether or not to approve a particular transfer. If the attacker controls most of these validators, they can approve fake and malicious transfers. In the Ronin Network hack, the attacker took over five of the bridge's nine validators.

A bridge hack can drain the liquidity and cause complex effects among different protocols, even the connected blockchain. So it requires multiple rigorous internal and external smart contract audits. Further, the cross-chain bridges must have strict internal security policies and educate the team about possible attack vectors. The Ronin Bridge was hacked because one employee was compromised under advanced spear-phishing attacks.

10. The Only Giant and Multi-great Power

At the beginning of 2020, Ethereum's fees were still friendly to most DeFi users. However, the rapid growths of TVL and new users in DeFi summer have led to the rise of gas fees, discouraging new users who have less capital. The speed of transactions of Ethereum is slow. These all led investors and developers to look for cheaper and faster alternatives. From the data in Fig. 5, we can intuitively see that the TVL proportion of Ethereum in the market continues to decline till the crash of Terra in mid-May.

According to the data from Blockchain-Comparison.com, as of August 6, 2022, there were 118 public blockchains in the market. Low transaction costs are the most crucial consideration for some users, and decentralization is not a priority. These allow EVM chains to develop. According to DefiLlama's data, BNB Chain, Polygon, and Avalanche are the leading EVM public blockchains at the top. In terms of the EVM public blockchain market, EVM Layer-1 blockchain grabbed about 25% of Ethereum's share from January to May 2021. However, as shown in Fig. 6, Ethereum's market share has been varying by around 75% since May 2021. Ethereum remains in the leading position.

According to Fig. 7, non-EVM Layer-1 blockchain grabbed about 35% of Ethereum's share by May 2022. After the crash of Terra, the market share of

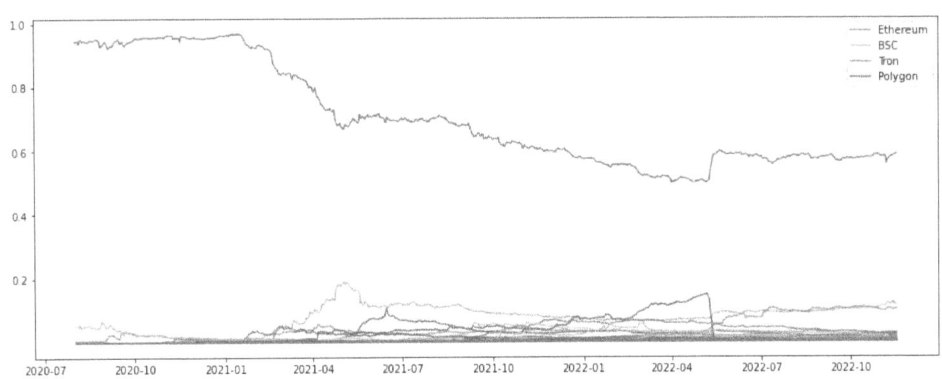

Fig. 5. (Color online) The proportion of TVLs.

Source: Retrieved from DefiLlama at: https://defillama.com/chains.

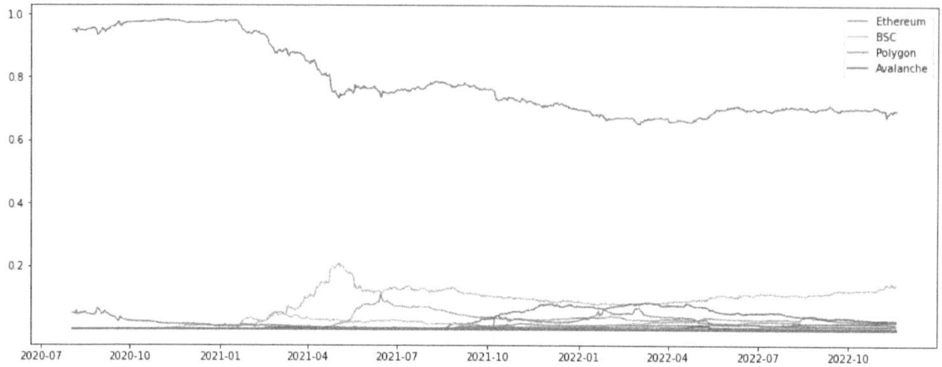

Fig. 6. (Color online) The proportions of TVLs of Ethereum and EVM Layer 1.
Source: Retrieved from DefiLlama at: https://defillama.com/chains/EVM.

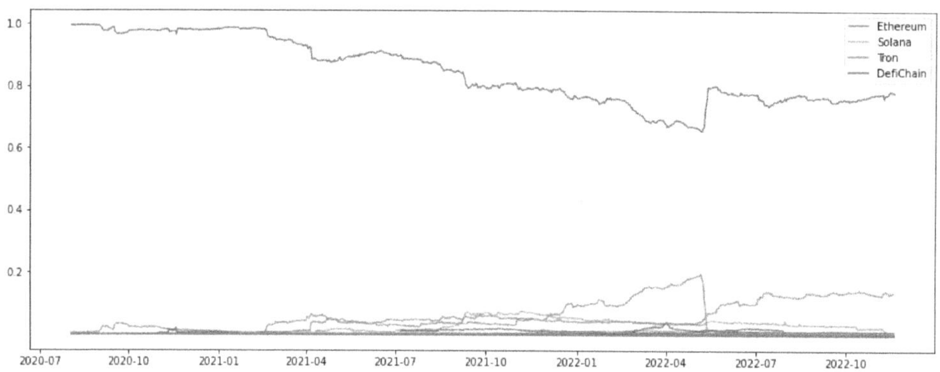

Fig. 7. (Color online) The proportions of TVLs of Ethereum and non-EVM Layer 1.
Source: Retrieved from DefiLlama at: https://defillama.com/chains/Non-EVM.

Ethereum varied between 75% and 80% till November 2022. With capital support, non-EVM chains such as Tron and Solana have seen significant growth in TVLs. The low gas fee has attracted many users who cannot afford high gas fees on Ethereum.

According to Fig. 8, we can see clearly that the ratio of Roll Up TVL to Ethereum TVL keeps increasing. With optimum token incentive plan and the continuous development of Arbitrum, zkSync, and Starknet ecology, it is highly possible for the TVL of Layer 2 to increase.

From the data in Fig. 8, Ethereum is underperforming based on TVL. However, the TVL on Ethereum is far superior to other public blockchains. Those important protocols are still running mainly on Ethereum. Thus, Ethereum will remain the first choice for excellent developers and be the most significant

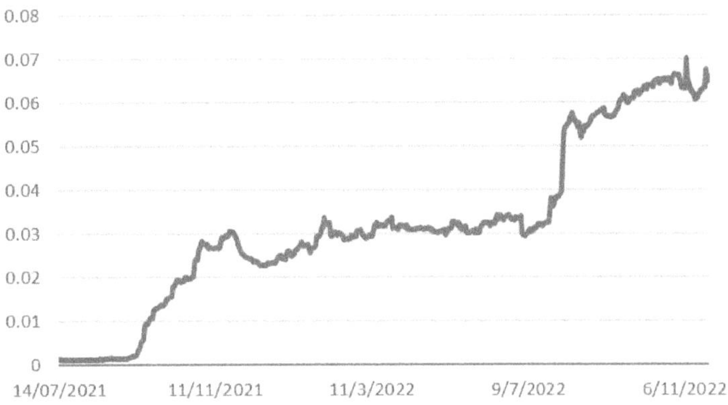

Fig. 8. Ratio of Roll Up TVL to Ethereum TVL.

Source: Retrieved from DefiLlama at: https://defillama.com/chains/Rollup.

blockchain for a long time. Other blockchains will grab this opportunity to develop into application-specific ones to occupy part of the market share. For example, Kava has developed into a financial blockchain. Avalanche and Wax have intensely cultivated games. Flow and Immutable focus on NFT. Aztec and Oasis provide privacy. The Metaverse offers a large market, and the future is a multi-chain pattern.

11. The Future of Cross-chain

11.1. *Source liquidity from existing DeFi protocols*

It is the most popular model nowadays that bridges have their Liquidity Pools. However, it is not capital-efficient. Further, decreasing the amount of money locked makes it less appealing for hackers to attack. Thus, cross-chain protocols may consider getting liquidity from current DeFi protocols. DeFi ecosystem can be more united and the flow of capital can be more efficient.

11.2. *Survival of the fittest*

Cross-chain is a lucrative business that handles billions of dollars in transaction volume. Many projects are competing to win. On the one hand, they will have to compete on fees. On the other hand, they will fight hackers. The bridge aggregators lead more users to bridges that provide the best service. Some users only use bridges that haven't issued tokens for the airdrop. We will see many uncompetitive protocols diminish gradually.

11.3. *Compensation fund against risk*

Cross-chain protocols may coordinate with insurance protocols or set up compensation funds to distribute the risk. Cross-chain protocols may cover the insurance fee for attracting users. Users can also pay the cost. It is the same logic as we buy traffic tickets.

11.4. *Composable infrastructure*

We will see more DeFi, NFT, and DAO built based on cross-chain messaging protocols to achieve composability and interoperability. The performance will be improved gradually. Cross-chain protocols will be the source of innovations.

12. Summary

In 2021, the major public blockchains saw significant advancements due to the support of investors and developers. Going forward, each blockchain will concentrate its efforts on a particular field that aligns with its unique mechanism. The establishment of the multi-chain world has made it difficult to reverse, and although it may pose potential risks, the cross-chain protocol connecting these isolated blockchains is crucial for its existence. We can expect to see an increase in cross-chain applications being developed in the future, taking advantage of the interoperability and composability between blockchains. These advancements are poised to bring new and exciting surprises and it is exciting to anticipate the infinite possibilities that interoperability offers.

References

Alo, 2022, Post Mortem Report — Meter Passport, *Medium*, February 19, available at: https://medium.com/meter-io/post-mortem-report-meter-passport-12af6b50393d.

Barrett, M., 2022, Harmony's Horizon Bridge Hack, *Medium*, June 24, available at: https://medium.com/harmony-one/harmonys-horizon-bridge-hack-1e8d283b6d66.

Behnke, R., 2022, What is a Cross-Chain Bridge and How are Bridges Hacked? *Halborn*, August 6, available at: https://halborn.com/what-is-a-cross-chain-bridge-and-how-are-bridges-hacked/.

Beosin, 2022a, H1 2022 Web3 Security Research, https://beosin.com/resources/Beosin_H1_2022_Web3_Security_Report.pdf.

Beosin, 2022b, BNB Chain's $850 Million Hack — Using Beosin Trace to Investigate the Stolen-Funds, October 9, available at: https://beosin.com/resources/bnb-chain%E2%80%99s-850-million-hack-beosin-trace-investigation.

Berenzon, D., 2021, Blockchain Bridges: Building Networks of Cryptonetworks, *Medium*, September 8, available at: https://medium.com/1kxnetwork/blockchain-bridges-5db6afac44f8.

Borkowski, M., C. Ritzer, D. McDonald, and S. Schulte, 2018b, Caught in Chains: Claim-First Transactions for Cross-Blockchain Asset Transfers, White Paper, August, TU Wien.

Borkowski, M., D. McDonald, C. Ritzer, and S. Schulte, 2018a, Towards Atomic Cross-Chain Token Transfers: State of the Art and Open Questions within TAST, White Paper, May, TU Wien.

Borkowski, M., P. Frauenthaler, M. Sigwart, T. Hukkinen, O. Hladky, and S. Schulte, 2019, Cross-Blockchain Technologies: Review, State of the Art, and Outlook, White Paper, March, TU Wien.

Buterin, V., 2022, Welcome to Reddit, *Reddit*, available at: https://old.reddit.com/r/ethereum/comments/rwojtk/ama_we_are_the_efs_research_team_pt_7_07_january/hrngyk8/.

Cardfarm, 2021, Cross-chain Bridges Explored, *Medium*, April 21, available at: https://medium.com/momentum6/cross-chain-bridges-explored-929e6b68dcd1.

Celer Network, 2021a, cBridge 2.0: Coherent Blockchain Interoperability Powered by the State Guardian Network, Blog, September 22, available at: https://blog.celer.network/2021/09/22/cbridge-2-0-coherent-blockchain-interoperability-powered-by-the-state-guardian-network/.

Celer Network, 2021b, cBridge 2.0 Mainnet Launch: The Next Step to a Seamless Interoperable Future, Blog, November 17, available at: https://blog.celer.network/2021/11/17/cbridge-2-0-mainnet-launch-the-next-step-to-a-seamless-interoperable-future/.

Celer Network, 2022a, Celer Inter-chain Message Framework: The Paradigm Shift for Building and Using Multi-blockchain dApps, Blog, January 12, available at: https://blog.celer.network/2022/01/12/celer-inter-chain-message-framework-the-paradigm-shift-for-building-and-using-multi-blockchain-dapps/.

Celer Network, 2022b, Celer IM Launches on Mainnet: A New Era for Inter-chain dApps Begins, Blog, April 25, available at: https://blog.celer.network/2022/04/25/celer-im-launches-on-mainnet-a-new-era-for-inter-chain-dapps-begins/.

Chainalysis, 2022, Vulnerabilities in Cross-chain Bridge Protocols Emerge as Top Security Risk, Blog, August 2, available at: https://blog.chainalysis.com/reports/cross-chain-bridge-hacks-2022/.

ChainSwap, 2021, ChainSwap Exploit 11 July 2021 Post-Mortem, Blog, July 12, available at: https://chain-swap.medium.com/chainswap-exploit-11-july-2021-post-mortem-6e4e346e5a32.

Cong, Z., Z. Liang, Y. Huang, F. Xiong, M. Qin, and Z. Guo, 2022, Research on Cross-chain Technology of Blockchain: Challenges and Prospects, in *Proceedings of the 2022 IEEE 2nd International Conference on Power, Electronics and Computer Applications (ICPECA)*, IEEE, Piscataway, pp. 422–428.

Deng, L., H. Chen, J. Zeng, and L.-J. Zhang, 2018, Research on Cross-chain Technology based on Sidechain and Hash-Locking, in S. Liu, B. Tekinerdogan, M. Aoyama and L. J. Zhang (editors), *Edge Computing — EDGE 2018*, Lecture Notes in Computer Science, Vol. 10973, Springer, Cham, pp. 144–151.

European Central Bank, 2021, The Use of DLT in Post-trade Processes, Working Paper, Working Groups on Market Infrastructures for Securities and Collateral and for Payments, April, available at: https://www.ecb.europa.eu/pub/pdf/other/ecb.20210412_useofdltposttradeprocesses~958e3af1c8.en.pdf.

Gu, Y., G. Sun, J. Wang, K. Liu, C. Zhou, and X. You, 2021, CISV: A Cross-Blockchain Information Synchronization and Verification Mode, in *FICC 2020: Intelligent Computing and Blockchain*, Communications in Computer and Information Science, Vol. 1385, Springer, Singapore, pp. 239–252.

John, J., 2022, Bridges — An Introduction, *Decentralised.co*, July 27, available at: https://www.decentralised.co/p/bridges-an-introduction.

Kan, L., Y. Wei, H. M. Amjad, S. Wang, L. C. Gao, and H. Kai, 2018, A Multiple Blockchains Architecture on Inter-Blockchain Communication, in *Proceedings of the 2018 IEEE International Conference on Software Quality, Reliability and Security Companion (QRS-C)*, IEEE.

Kannengieseer, N., M. Pfister, M. Greulich, S. Lins, and A. Sunyeav, 2020, Bridges between Islands: Cross-Chain Technology for Distributed Ledger Technology, in *Proceedings of the 53rd Hawaii International Conference on System Sciences*, Association for Information System, pp. 5298–5307.

Kwon, J. and E. Buchman, 2016, Cosmos: A Network of Distributed Ledgers, White Paper, available at: https://v1.cosmos.network/resources/whitepaper.

Lee, D. K. C. (editor), 2020, *Artificial Intelligence, Data and Blockchain in a Digital Economy*, 1st edition, Singapore University of Social Sciences-World Scientific Future Economy Series, Vol. 3, World Scientific, Singapore.

Nomad Bridge, 2022, Nomad Bridge Hack: Root Cause Analysis, *Medium*, August 5, available at: https://medium.com/nomad-xyz-blog/nomad-bridge-hack-root-cause-analysis-875ad2e5aacd.

Ou, W., S. Li, H. Li, Y. Wang, L. Liu, H. Zhang, and X. Li, 2022, Performance Modeling and Evaluation of the Inter-Blockchain Network: A Queuing Approach, Working Paper, Social Science Research Network, doi:10.2139/ssrn.4043298.

Ronin Network, 2022, Community Alert: Ronin Validators Compromised, *Ronin's Newsletter*, March 29, available at: https://roninblockchain.substack.com/p/community-alert-ronin-validators.

Simpier, D., 2022, Everything You Need to Know about the Gravity Bridge Chain, Blog, March 3, available at: https://blog.cosmos.network/gravity-is-an-essential-force-of-the-cosmos-aligning-all-planets-in-orbits-in-the-composable-b1ca17de18cc.

SlowMist, 2021, The Root Cause of Poly Network Being Hacked, *Medium*, August 11, available at: https://slowmist.medium.com/the-root-cause-of-poly-network-being-hacked-ec2ee1b0c68f.

SlowMist, 2022a, Our Analysis of the $80M Qubit Finance Exploit, *Medium*, January 29, available at: https://slowmist.medium.com/our-analysis-of-the-80m-qubit-finance-exploit-b0f272cd8c25.

SlowMist, 2022b, Cross-chain DEX Aggregator Transit Swap Hacked Analysis, *Medium*, October 2, available at: https://slowmist.medium.com/cross-chain-dex-aggregator-transit-swap-hacked-analysis-74ba39c22020.

Tendermint, Inc., 2022, What is Cosmos?, *Cosmos*, available at: https://v1.cosmos.network/intro.

Tremback, J., 2021, How Gravity Works, *Althea*, February 25, available at: https://blog.althea.net/how-gravity-works/.

Tsepeleva, R. and V. Korkhov, 2021, Implementation of the Cross-Blockchain Interacting Protocol, in *ICCSA 2021: Computational Science and Its Applications*, Lecture Notes in Computer Science, Vol. 12952, Springer, Singapore, pp. 42–55.

Wood, G., 2018, Ethereum: A Secure Decentralized Generalized Transaction Ledger, Working Paper, Berlin Version, October 24, available at: https://ethereum.github.io/yellowpaper/paper.pdf.

Wormhole, 2022, Wormhole Incident Report — 02/02/22, *Medium*, February 5, available at: https://wormholecrypto.medium.com/wormhole-incident-report-02-02-22-ad9b8f21eec6.

Zarick, R., 2021a, The Bridging Trilemma, *Medium*, October 29, available at: https://medium.com/stargate-official/the-bridging-trilemma-d80788cce4ef.

Zarick, R., 2021b, LayerZero — An Omnichain Interoperability Protocol, *Medium*, September 16, available at: https://medium.com/layerzero-official/layerzero-an-omnichain-interoperability-protocol-b43d2ae975b6.

Zarick, R., B. Pellegrino, and C. Banister, 2021, Solving the Bridging Trilemma, *Dropbox*, https://www.dropbox.com/s/gf3606jedromp61/Delta-Solving. The.Bridging-Trilemma.pdf?dl=0.

Zuo, Y. X., M. Yang, Z. P. Qiang, D. Fei, X. F. Shao, S. Q. Su, Q. Mo, and Z. H. Liang, 2022, A Review of Cross-Blockchain Solutions, in *CloudComp 2021: Cloud Computing*, Lecture Notes of the Institute for Computer Sciences, Social Informatics and Telecommunications Engineering, Vol. 430, Springer, Singapore, pp. 221–233.

Appendix A. A Case Study to Demonstrate the Design Thinking for Cross-chain Aggregation and Associated Technology

In this appendix, we use a case study on Chainge to demonstrate a way to resolving the Bridging Trilemma in the DeFi space. This is a difficult problem to solve but Chainge provided a design to overcome the vulnerabilities of cross-chain transactions. The purpose is not understanding the design thinking underlying the aggregator.

Chainge.finance[13] is the first[14] real cross-chain liquidity aggregator in operation. A good way to differentiate between their model and other self-proclaimed cross-chain aggregators is to follow the transactional path of a specific swap. While other aggregators access liquidity from one single chain per transaction, Chainge's smart router is able to split transactions into fractions on multiple chains, thus accessing the liquidity sum from all chains for any given trade.

Chainge's DEX is built on the Fusion blockchain, the same blockchain on which Multichain (formerly known as AnySwap) was originally developed. Chainge uses the same Fusion DCRM tech but takes it a wide step forward. Chainge provides broad access to DeFi, across the cross-chain ecosystem, through a straightforward and user-centric mobile-native application. The Chainge DEX aggregates liquidity across various chains and DEXs, enabling easy cross-chain interoperability in a decentralized, non-custodial fashion.

Chainge offers a mobile application aiming to simplify the user experience with DeFi with a focus on cross-chain interoperability and chain-agnostic assets, aiming to help users abstract away the complexity of interacting between disparate blockchains with incompatible state machines while providing the benefits of liquidity and DeFi offerings split across chains.

Chainge's mobile app focuses heavily on providing a better UX for cross-chain swaps (i.e. one that doesn't require users to manually check prices on various DEXs, navigate bridges, or switch between wallets).

In addition, Chainge offers a wide array of decentralized services including the following:

1. A self-custodial Cross-chain Wallet for users to store, send, and receive assets across multiple networks. It is a Futures DEX and the first decentralized Options DEX for users to get the best prices and discover the derivatives market.
2. Decentralized staking also known as Time Framing and Liquidity Pools to generate daily passive income with no worries and no hassle.

---

[13]Official website of Chainge.finance, https://www.chainge.finance/.

[14]Terminology here is debatable since "cross-chain" liquidity aggregators traditionally denominate an aggregator that can perform cross-chain swaps, meaning that they aggregate single chain liquidity and then bridge the assets post-swap. Meanwhile in Chainge's case, "cross-chain liquidity aggregator" implies an aggregator that can actually access cross-chain liquidity. They underline this difference by more accurately naming the first category "multi-chain aggregators". See, for more details, https://twitter.com/FinanceChainge/status/1530963085753823234?s=20&t=pe0rurfFAIr3qogZQZre_g.

3. Escrow Smart Contracts for users to safely buy and sell goods or services and trade crypto-OTC.
4. Decentralized perpetuals.

Despite an easy-to-use mobile app, Chainge isn't just targeting retail users. One major selling point for Chainge is, perhaps, the underlying blockchain's gearing toward enterprise and institutional adoption, while also affording users' control over their assets.

A.1. *Technology*

A.1.1. *Fusion blockchain*

Chainge is built on an EVM-compatible, finance-focused public blockchain called Fusion. To Fusion's credit, rather than waiting for Ethereum to solve its own proof-of-stake design, Fusion was operating a PoS network in the summer of 2019 along with other specific fit-for-purpose alterations. Because Fusion is an Ethereum fork, nearly all Ethereum-specific tools are compatible with Fusion. Important developer tooling, infrastructure, and user-facing products, such as the popular Web wallet Metamask, can be simply modified to work with Fusion. Since Ethereum and Fusion addresses are identical, migrating from Ethereum to Fusion is a simple process.

Fusion represents a permutation on a proof-of-stake network with token rewards based on participating in staking via a Ticketed Proof of Stake (TPoS) consensus mechanism. TPoS involves buying tickets to potentially be given the right to generate the next block. Please refer Fig. A.1. to see how Fusion exchanges

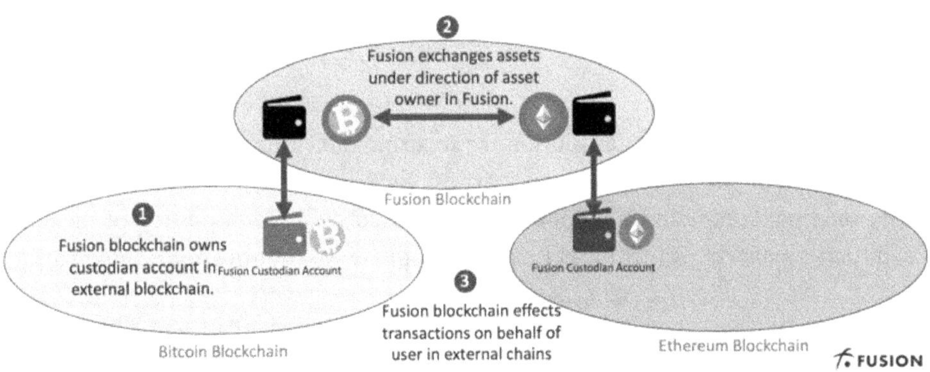

Fig. A.1. An interoperable solution at the asset encryption level that does not impose compatibility standards.

assets between blockchains. It's essentially a lottery where "5,000 FSNs purchase a ticket for a chance to win a block with their anonymous node".

Fusion aims to facilitate interoperability between chains via a network of custodial wallets on various chains. When Fusion initially launched DCRM in 2019, it was in a beta test environment comprised of five organizations and 29 community nodes. Now, as of Q1 2023, Fusion has 64 validators.

A.2. *Fusion Distributed Control Rights Management approach*

The Fusion DCRM technology aims to solve some of the centralization concerns related to private key management via a "distributed key generation and signing algorithm". Fusion was made with the backing of various academic cryptographers[15] (Rosario Gennaro, Professor of Computer Science at CUNY; Steven Goldfeder, Ph.D., Postdoctoral Researcher in the Department of Computer Science at Cornell University; Louis Goubin, Professor of Computer Science at University of Versailles; and Pascal Paillier, Ph.D., CEO and Senior Security Expert at CryptoExperts) and involves technologies, such as MPC and TSS.

A.3. *DCRM*

DCRM creates a decentralized custodian model that leverages multi-party sign-offs for smart contract transactions by allowing multiple nodes in a network to share access permissions for wallets or other sensitive information. The Fusion blockchain uses shared storage of private keys in which the key is broken into parts and distributed across nodes in the network, such that the private key isn't recoverable in any one place. Table A.1. offers a comparison of signature.

A.4. *MPC*

Multi-party Computation is a solution for securing data among several participants in a private manner. It allows many parties, each with their own private data, to verify the final computation without revealing their own secret portion of the data. Each participant in an MPC possesses a piece of confidential information.

[15] For more details, see "World-Class Cryptographers Join Forces with Fusion to Build Superior Blockchain Interoperability and Distributed Custodial Solution", available at: https://www.globenewswire.com/news-release/2019/04/08/1798925/0/en/World-Class-Cryptographers-Join-Forces-with-Fusion-to-Build-Superior-Blockchain-Interoperability-and-Distributed-Custodial-Solution.html.

Table A.1. Comparison of signature.

Cryptography	Private key signature	Multi-signature	Distributed signature
Encryption Scheme	public key encryption	public key encryption	public key encryption
Cryptography Algorithm	ECC	ECC, MultiSig	ECC, DKG, Paillier encryption, zero-knowledge proof, threshold signature
Decentralization Degree	centralization	multi-centered	decentralization
Cross-chain Support	Not supported	Not supported	supported
Implementation Difficulties	Low	Medium	High
Safety Provability	Yes	Yes	Yes
Realization Projects	Bitcoin/Ethereum etc	Bitcoin/Ethereum etc	FUSION

Typically, in the case of bridges, one entity owns one part of a cryptographic key that can move funds or change code.

MPCs are (generally) used when a bridging system has multiple and/or a permissionless Relayer set and is looking to eliminate one bad actor as a single point of failure. MPCs shared a private key into many segments, with each individual possessing a portion of the private key. When signing a transaction, a subset of MPC nodes must independently sign the transaction and communicate it to the larger group.

Even if a bridging protocol has a limited quantity of Relayer nodes, the Relayers can be chosen at random from the pool of candidates to create the MPC group. To authorize a cross-chain transaction, the protocol can require a minimum number of Relayers to come together and sign the message before any action can be taken. The greater the threshold of an MPC group, the less likely it is that Relayer groups will collude.

MPC also guarantees that if a number of parties inside the group decide to disclose information or depart from the protocol's instructions during execution, the MPC will not allow them to coerce the honest parties into outputting an inaccurate result or leaking confidential information.

Fusion's DCRM Alliance is the primary MPC participant. Each Alliance member operates their own off-chain node that functions solely to maintain custody of assets during cross-chain bridging. With the combination of the Fusion chain and the Alliance, the protocol stores assets on various external blockchains.

When individuals wish to transfer their assets, the Fusion chain uses these external wallets to transfer the funds to the user. With different nodes managed by multiple individuals, there is no central authority, and no one member can act without consent from the others.

A.5. *TSS*

TSS involve a subset of trusted nodes participating in key generation and signature events. MPC requires that more than one entity/node/validator is necessary to control the wallet's contents. TSS are a subset of MPC. TSS enable multiple entities to collaboratively generate a key and a signature rather than just one party. After the key is generated, no single entity ever has access to the full key and can't sign without the cooperation of the others. TSS consist of two values: n and t, where n is the number of nodes required to generate a signature, and t is the total number of entities involved. Fig. A.2. shows the structure of threshold signature schemes.

The benefits of TSS over simple multi-sig configurations are as follows:

1. Multi-sig configurations perform their cryptography on-chain, exposing details, such as the number of signers that weaken security.
2. TSS signatures are treated as one signature on the blockchain, making the costs of TSS signatures much cheaper.

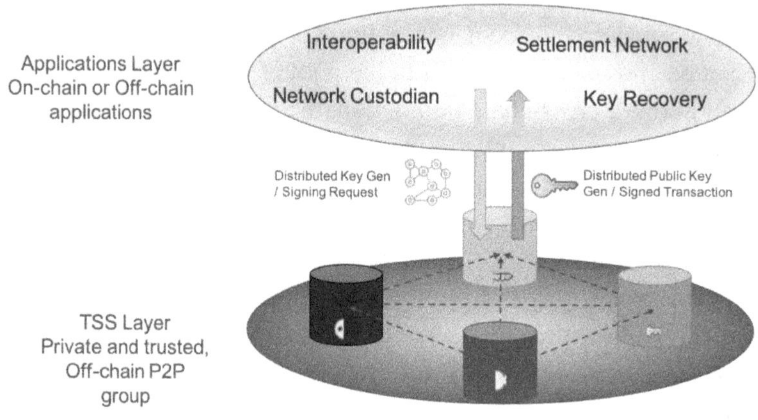

Fig. A.2. The structure of Threshold Signature Schemes.

A.6. *Chainge's value propositions*

A.6.1. *Cross-chain liquidity aggregation*

Chainge's technology stack and design choices are based around abstracting away the complexities of crypto-key management and crypto-bridging. The mobile application serves as a DeFi hub that can interact with 38 blockchains and 1,500+ crypto-assets in one easy-to-use interface. Users of Chainge can move freely across the crypto-ecosystem in just a few taps as opposed to multiple wallets, chains, bridges, and seed phrases, all while tapping into more than $60 billion in liquidity across dozens of chains.

Behind the simple interface, Chainge provides truly cross-chain, simultaneous trades with the deepest liquidity. Chainge acts as a cross-chain DEX aggregator as well as an aggregator of DEX aggregators, as they announced an integration with 1inch in June of 2022 with others subsequently following.

Once a user initiates a transaction via the Chainge app, on the back end, Chainge searches the top DEXs on the biggest blockchains and pulls liquidity from multiple chains simultaneously for one single transaction that sees it's finality in a matter of minutes.

Large trades are split across different blockchains to take advantage of multiple liquidity sources in order to reduce slippage. As a result, the Chainge router, within its DEX aggregator, determines the optimal path to the most liquidities and lowest prices.

A.6.2. *Cross-chain roaming also known as multi-cross-chain transactions*

Another additional feature that separates Chainge from traditional bridges or interoperability models is its "universal/chain-agnostic asset" feature. With Chainge, tokens from multiple disparate networks can be bridged to one destination chain with one (user) transaction, i.e. bridging USDT from 10 different chains to Solana at the same time within minutes, as opposed to 10 individual bridging transactions.

Chainge implements the "bridge" function via the "relay chain mode", with Fusion being the relay chain. No matter how many steps a bridge order has, the core steps come in pairs: wrap-in and wrap-out. A relay chain makes a very complicated multi-bridge path (such as the one above) simple.

This in turn also helps users swap their assets regardless on how many chains they are spread across with one tap in the Chainge Finance app.

As opposed to currently available lacking interoperability solutions, by widely adopting Chainge's cross-chain liquidity aggregation solution, the Bridging Trilemma the DeFi space is currently facing would be permanently resolved as per the following facts:

1. There are no limitations to the number of chains or assets the Chainge ecosystem could integrate (powered by Fusion DCRM tech).
2. Chainge unifies liquidity across chains while providing almost instant finality to bridging operations.
3. Users can move their assets to their native chains as preferred within minutes.

A Commentary on "Voting Schemes in DAO Governance"

Daniel Liebau

Department of Finance at Rotterdam School of Management,
Erasmus University, The Netherlands
liebau@rsm.nl

1. Introduction

The original article "Voting Schemes in DAO Governance" by Ding *et al.* (2023) provides a comprehensive overview of current voting mechanisms in DAOs and proposes a novel one. This commentary offers an update on the rapidly evolving literature surrounding the DAO ecosystem, focusing on governance and voting in particular. Several noteworthy contributions have further expanded our understanding of DAO governance dynamics in the months following Ding *et al.*'s publication. I aim to extend the original article's value by highlighting recent theoretical and empirical advancements in the field. Specifically, I showcase new perspectives on centralization forces in DAOs, innovative methods for measuring decentralization, and empirical insights into delegation patterns and the relationship between governance structures and governance token performance in markets. I designed this commentary to complement the original work by Ding *et al.*, and readers are encouraged to refer to both the original article and the additional references discussed herein for a deeper understanding of the topics.

2. Review

2.1. *Theory*

Bakos and Halaburda (2023) find that while blockchain technologies aim to enable decentralization and self-governance, the tradability of DAO governance tokens tends to centralize control over time, challenging true decentralization. This finding is crucial because most governance tokens are tradable, and the issue persists even when tokens are initially widely distributed. Concentrated holdings of governance tokens by large venture capital investors exacerbate this problem. These centralization forces raise critical questions: Do they undermine DAOs' initial value proposition of removing costly intermediaries? Are traditional intermediaries preferable since we can at least identify them, unlike some actors within DAOs?

2.2. *Voting-Bloc Entropy*

Austgen *et al.* (2023) propose a new metric, Voting-Bloc Entropy (VBE), which represents a significant innovation in measuring decentralization in DAOs. The key idea behind VBE is to assess centralization based on tokens held by groups of DAO members with aligned interests rather than individual token holders. This approach departs from traditional methods that measure token distribution across individual addresses. VBE focuses on how tokens are distributed across blocs of voters with the same incentives, treating these blocs as functionally single entities. VBE provides insights into the effects of various governance mechanisms on decentralization, including vote delegation, proposal bundling, bribery, and quadratic voting. This nuanced approach offers a more accurate picture of a DAO's actual level of decentralization, making it a valuable tool for both researchers and practitioners in the field of DAO governance. This metric is crucial in understanding and designing more effective and genuinely decentralized governance systems in the future.

2.3. *Empirics*

Fritsch *et al.* (2022) were the first to investigate the role of delegation in DAOs at a high level. Their data show that most voting power lies in the hands of a few delegates, who often receive their voting power from a single token holder. This finding underscores the urgent need for further research into delegation patterns and their implications for DAO governance. Appel and Grennan (2023) find that governance aspects promoting broad participation and security correlate with positive abnormal returns in DAO governance tokens, while barriers to adopting improvement proposals are linked to negative abnormal returns. These insights can also guide those considering engaging with DAOs, whether as customers, service providers, or investors.

3. Conclusion and Outlook

The current state of DAO governance and voting presents numerous research opportunities that could potentially reshape our understanding of these systems. Key questions remain: Can we confirm the theoretical findings of centralization forces when analyzing current DAO data? What would an empirical analysis using voting-bloc entropy reveal about voter alignment? How do these measures evolve over time? Additionally, connecting empirical findings by Fritsch *et al.* to finance theory could illuminate differences between traditional firms and DAOs in financial markets. What can off-chain data teach us about DAO governance processes? We are only at the beginning of the research journey into DAO governance and voting, and the potential impact of these investigations is both exciting and significant. Conferences like dawo24.org, held this year in Winterthur, Switzerland, and organized by Florian Spychiger, Michael Lustenberger, Sabrina Wollenschlaeger, and Lukas Kueng, will contribute significantly to our understanding of these phenomena in the future.

References

Appel, I. and Grennan, J., 2023. Decentralized Governance and Digital Asset Prices. *Working paper*. https://papers.ssrn.com/sol3/papers.cfm?abstract_id=4367209.

Austgen, J., Fabrega, A., Allen, S., Babel, K., Kelkar, M., and Juels, A., 2023. DAO decentralization: Voting-Bloc entropy, bribery, and dark DAOs. arXiv electronic journal. https://arxiv.org/abs/2311.03530.

Bakos, Y. and Halaburda, H., 2023. Will Blockchains Disintermediate Platforms? The Problem of Credible Decentralization in DAOs. *Working paper.* https://papers.ssrn.com/sol3/papers.cfm?abstract_id=4221512.

Ding, Q., Xu, W., Wang, Z., and Lee, D., 2023. Voting schemes in DAO Governance. *Annual Review of Fintech*. https://www.worldscientific.com/doi/10.1142/S2811004823500045.

Fritsch, R., Muller, M., and Wattenhofer, R., 2022. Analyzing Voting Power in Decentralized Governance: Who Controls DAOs? *Working Paper*. https://arxiv.org/abs/2204.01176.

Voting Schemes in DAO Governance*

Qinxu Ding, Weibiao Xu, Zhiguo Wang and
David Kuo Chuen Lee†

School of Business, Singapore University of Social Sciences
Singapore 599494, Singapore
†*davidleekc@suss.edu.sg*

This paper aims to provide a comprehensive overview of the different voting schemes used in DAO governance. We will examine the various features of these schemes and compare their differences. We propose a new hypothetical voting mechanism specifically designed for decentralized and permissionless DAO governance. This new scheme, which incorporates incentive designs, is intended to be more efficient than existing schemes and can be easily adapted to a permissioned scenario. Through this examination and proposal, we hope to contribute to the ongoing discourse on how to govern decentralized autonomous organizations effectively.

Keywords: Voting process; DAO; governance.

1. Introduction

A decentralized autonomous organization (DAO) is an emerging legal organization structure (El Faqir *et al.*, 2020; Hassan and De Filippi, 2021). It is not controlled by a single entity such as a government or central bank. It is decentralized among various members, such as computers, networks, and nodes. In contrast, governance used to be a concept in a centralized manner. It is to reflect some parties' decisions or views on others. A DAO is run according to computer codes

---

*This Chapter was originally published in the *World Scientific Annual Review of Fintech*, Vol. 1, No. 1, doi: 10.1142/S2811004823500045.

†Corresponding author.

rather than by a group of individuals. The rules and processes of the organization are encoded into a smart contract and are executed automatically. Typically, DAOs are decentralized and run on blockchain networks, meaning that they operate autonomously and are not controlled by a central authority.

On the other hand, governance refers to the process by which decisions are made, and rules are established in an organization. For blockchain and cryptocurrency, governance often refers to the process by which changes to a blockchain protocol or the rules of a cryptocurrency are proposed, debated, and implemented. This can include changes to the consensus algorithm, the addition of new features, or the allocation of funds. In summary, a DAO is a type of organization that is wholly run by a smart contract, whereas governance is the process of decision-making and rule-making for an organization. DAOs can use governance to make decisions. The way to embed the governance component into a DAO is a crucial issue and this must be decided initially. The governance scheme should incentivize the members to achieve a common goal to improve the DAO.

Current literature in management is mainly focusing on the relationship between DAOs and corporate governance. For example, many studies investigate how DAO could transform and improve corporate governance (Yermack, 2017; Kaal, 2021; Morrison *et al.*, 2020). But we believe DAO governance *per se* is an interesting topic to investigate. DAO governance represents a new paradigm in organizational management, that is self-governance with a bunch of self-executed rules. The mechanism to achieve an agreement among humans in a democratically governed system is through voting and with the aim of reducing the centralization feature of governance (Zhao *et al.*, 2022), allowing for a more equitable distribution of power among stakeholders.

In computer science, voting schemes are often studied under the subfields of cryptography, distributed systems, and algorithm design. They mainly focus on the concerns related to security or privacy for the voting designs (Chaum, 1981; Benaloh, 1987; Boyd, 1990; Fujioka *et al.*, 1993; Sako and Killian, 1995; Cramer *et al.*, 1997; Jakobsson *et al.*, 2002, Neff, 2004; Sampigethaya and Poovendran, 2006; Ribeiro and Joaquim, 2012). For example, Neff (2004) introduces the MarkPldege (MP) technique to provide high "vote encryption assurance" to the voter. His research aims to assure the voter that the vote is encrypted.[1] Encrypting

[1] Vote encryption assurance, also known as end-to-end verifiable voting, is a method used to ensure the privacy and integrity of voting in electronic voting systems. It involves encrypting the votes before they are cast, and then decrypting them only after the voting period has ended. This allows for the voter to verify that their vote has been correctly recorded, while also maintaining the anonymity of their vote. It also allows for the public to verify that the vote counting was done correctly

the votes ensures that they cannot be tampered with or changed during the voting period and makes it impossible to link a voter with their vote. This is important for maintaining the integrity of the voting process and ensuring that the results accurately reflect the will of the voters. Ribeiro and Joaquim (2012) extended and developed MarkPledge3 (MP3) to allow the voter to verify that her vote is correctly encrypted.

The existing discussions are either on the comparison between DAO governance and corporate governance or on specific technological implementations. However, there is little research covering efficiency, fairness, and self-motivated designs in the voting process mechanism. We fill the gap by looking into the practical voting schemes that are widely used in real applications and try to propose a new scheme from the perspective of design thinking.

2. DAO Voting Mechanisms

This section will review prevailing voting schemes used in DAO platforms. There are many types of practical voting schemes available in the DAO industry. Specifically, we will cover eight prevailing voting schemes: Token-based Quorum Voting, Quadratic Voting, Weighted Voting and Reputation-based Voting, Knowledge-extractable Voting (KEV), Multisig Voting, Holographic Consensus, Conviction Voting, and Rage Quitting Voting. A simple comparison will be presented at the end.

2.1. *Token-based quorum voting*

Quorum voting is a commonly used mechanism in DAO governance. For any given proposal, the participating voters in the voting process must exceed the certain pre-set threshold (e.g., 50% or 60%) of the total voters, or else the proposal will automatically be rejected. The threshold could vary according to protocols. After passing the threshold requirement or quorum, the proposal with higher votes will be approved. This ensures that a sufficient number of voters are participating in the decision-making process and also ensures that any proposal that is approved has the support of a significant portion of the community.

This threshold can vary depending on the specific protocol. One of the advantages of this protocol is that it allows a proposal to be approved even if voter

without exposing the individual votes. The use of encryption in voting systems is a key component in ensuring the security and transparency of the voting process.

turnout is low, as long as a sufficient number of voters support the proposal, unlike the quorum voting. This protocol is used by several DAOs such as Compound, Curve, and Kleros, and it is gaining popularity due to its simplicity and the fact that it doesn't require reaching a quorum.

The threshold could be measured in terms of tokens, where voters must hold a certain amount of tokens to be eligible to vote, or it could be measured in terms of voter participation, where a certain percentage of eligible voters must participate in the voting process for a proposal to be considered. While pure token-based voting is a popular voting scheme in DAO governance, it has some issues. The major one is that voters who hold more tokens than others could dominate the decision-making process, effectively giving them a disproportionate amount of influence. Additionally, the participant threshold required for this protocol can be costly and time-consuming as it requires a high voter turnout each time a proposal is put forward. Moreover, it is controversial to determine the optimal threshold level because an improper threshold will make the proposal too easy or too difficult to pass. Setting the threshold too high can make the decision-making process too restrictive, potentially leading to good proposals being rejected. On the other hand, setting the threshold too low can result in low-quality proposals being approved. It's important to find a balance in setting the threshold level to ensure that the decision-making process is fair and effective.

KyberDAO and Aave are examples adopting this voting scheme (Table 1).

2.2. *Quadratic voting*

Vitalik Buterin, the co-founder of Ethereum, has proposed a quadratic voting scheme as an alternative to the traditional "1 token 1 vote" and "1 person 1 vote" models. Unlike "1 token 1 vote" which gives a proportional voting power based

Table 1. Examples for the applications of token-based quorum voting.

Examples	Description
KyberDAO	KyberDAO is a decentralized exchange that allows users to trade cryptocurrencies. The platform operates through a DAO, in which token holders can vote on proposals related to the development and governance of the platform. The KyberDAO held the first public poll for the community on collecting the design of voting quorum/thresholds and participation incentivization methods.
Aave	Aave is a decentralized lending and borrowing platform that operates through a DAO. Token holders can vote on proposals related to the management and development of the platform. The number of votes required to pass a proposal is based on the number of tokens held by each voter.

on the number of tokens held and "1 person 1 vote" which allocates a single unit of voting power to each voter, quadratic voting allows voters to express the intensity of their preferences by allocating multiple units of voting power to a single proposal. This approach aims to strike a balance between giving each voter equal representation while also taking into account the economic stake that a voter holds in the DAO, and the level of importance they assign to a particular proposal.

Under the quadratic scheme, voters can buy tokens and use those tokens to gain greater voting power (Quarfoot *et al.*, 2017). The scheme allows each voter to vote on the same proposals with multiple voting power but tries to avoid monopoly from single token holders. The voting power is increased by the square of the number of tokens, i.e., it needs N^2 for N votes from the same voter. For example, one vote needs one token. If the voter wants one more vote, it needs $2^2 = 4$ tokens. So the voting power is the square root of the token. It is costly for a single voter to dominate the voting process.

The quadratic voting scheme has several advantages over traditional voting mechanisms. This approach addresses some of the issues from traditional token-based voting, such as the potential for larger token holders to dominate the decision-making process and allows for a more nuanced representation of preferences. One of the main advantages is that it incentivizes voters to only vote on proposals that they are truly passionate about, as the cost of voting increases with the number of votes cast. This helps to avoid the problem of voters casting votes on proposals they are not truly invested in, which can lead to poor decision-making. Additionally, by allowing voters to express the intensity of their preferences, it helps to protect the voting rights of minorities, and ensures that even small groups can have a significant impact on governance.

However, there are also some potential downsides to this approach. One of the main criticisms is that voting power is still a function of wealth, which could lead to plutocracy, or rule by the wealthy. This is not in line with the principle of radical democracy that is often associated with blockchain technology. Moreover, this scheme needs a mechanism to verify the voter. Otherwise, a simple Sybil attack by bots or faking multiple identities will adversely affect the voting.

Gitcoin and BrightID (Table 2) are examples that adopted this voting scheme.

2.3. *Weighted voting and reputation-based voting*

Weighted voting refers to a voting system where each voter has a certain number of votes they can cast, and the weight of each vote is determined by the number of votes a voter has. This means that a voter with more votes has a greater influence on the outcome of the vote compared to a voter with fewer votes.

Table 2. Examples for the applications of quadratic voting.

Examples	Description
Gitcoin	Gitcoin is a decentralized platform for funding open-source projects. Gitcoin uses QV for its quadratic funding mechanism, which allocates funds to projects based on the number of votes they receive from individual contributors. Contributors can allocate a budget of votes to different projects, with the number of votes for each project being the square root of the budget allocated.
BrightID	BrightID is a decentralized identity verification platform that aims to prevent sybil attacks (i.e., the creation of multiple fake identities) on decentralized networks. BrightID has incorporated quadratic voting into its platform to help incentivize users to participate in verification activities. In BrightID's quadratic voting system, users are given a certain number of tokens (called "Bright Tokens") that they can use to vote on proposals related to identity verification activities.

Reputation-based voting, on the other hand, is a voting system where the weight of a voter's vote is determined by their reputation or trustworthiness within the community. Voters are assigned a certain amount of reputation or influence based on factors such as their past contributions to the DAO, their level of engagement, or sometimes their stake in the DAO. This means that voters who are deemed more trustworthy or have a higher reputation within the community have a greater influence on the outcome of the vote compared to those with a lower reputation. This voting scheme usually weighs voters by considering the contributions a voter made rather than pure token holdings. Specifically, the voters with a track record are rewarded with a portable reputation, and the reputation will put more weight on their votes.

Under this mechanism, reputation instead of wealth has a significant effect. Track record is one measure of reputation. The length of time that users hold specific tokens could be also considered a measure of reputation or conviction or the alignment of interests. Reputation is like a credit accumulated by a timing process or contributions to DAO community. It is less likely to be transferred or traded. The reputation could be dynamic. For example, reputation could expire or diminish with time to avoid the effects of early easy-gainers and maintain fairness to all voters.

The weighted voting and reputation voting increase the difficulty of Sybil attacks, although the risk still exists. It is relatively more efficient and sustainable than token-based voting. Nevertheless, it could be challenging to build up a proper reputation system (Zhuang *et al.*, 2019). BPC DAO and OrangeDAO (Table 3) are examples of adopting a reputation-based voting system.[2]

[2] Ndau aims to be the world's first adaptive digital currency, designed with a goal of a long-term store of value with staking income.

Table 3. Examples for the applications of weighted voting and reputation-based voting.

Examples	Description
BPC DAO	The BPC DAO Voting Portal is an online application powered by Web3, which is being used by the BPC DAO to involve Ndau[2] holders in shaping the future of Ndau. Using this portal, all Ndau holders can suggest novel proposals and cast their votes on existing ones. The voting power of participants is calculated based on the amount of Ndau they own and their currency seat status, which is explained in the Ndau whitepaper. The voting process is designed to be weighted appropriately to guarantee equitable representation of all contributors.
OrangeDAO	OrangeDAO is collaborating with Snapshot to bring reputation-based voting to life. Snapshot has expansive DAO voting dataset while OrangeDAP has the capabilities to produce customizable reputation reports, resumes and NFTs. The combination can act as algorithm providers to create voting structures that more accurately reflect the sentiment of the community.

2.4. *Knowledge-extractable voting*

KEV is a type of voting system in which the knowledge or expertise of voters is taken into account when determining the outcome of a vote. This can be done by allowing voters to indicate their level of expertise on a given subject, or by using algorithms to assess the quality of their contributions to a discussion or debate.

The goal of KEV is to ensure that decisions are made based on the collective wisdom of the group, rather than just the preferences of a small number of individuals. This voting scheme can be used in a variety of contexts, including online communities, DAOs, and other forms of collective decision-making. This KEV scheme tries to allocate more weight to the vote from more knowledgeable experts. Under this scheme, the proposals will be categorized into different areas. Each area has a representative token. The token can be used to enhance the effect of the votes by putting more weight. In other words, the final voting outcome depends on a weighted average of the votes by using the knowledge tokens as weights.

KEV provides incentive schemes for voters to vote based on their expertise. The voters who use knowledge tokens as weights will be rewarded with more tokens if the proposal is passed. However, the tokens held will be reduced if the proposal fails. Therefore, voters without sufficient knowledge to judge the proposal are discouraged from voting. The knowledge tokens could not be transferred or traded. So, voters could not manage their voting effects by loopholes or other mechanisms that allowed them to increase their knowledge tokens.

This scheme is newly designed[3] and receiving attention in the industry. DIT Protocol (Decentralized Information Theory) is an example of using this voting scheme.[4] It is a decentralized protocol that aims to incentivize the creation and sharing of knowledge, by allowing users to vote on the quality and relevance of information. It is based on a reputation-based system, where users acquire reputation points by contributing valuable information, and can then use these points to vote on the relevance of other users' submissions. The DIT Protocol is intended to provide a decentralized and self-governing platform for knowledge sharing, where users can collectively curate and organize information.

2.5. *The multisig voting*

Multisig voting is a voting mechanism where multiple signatures or approvals are required before a proposal can be executed. It is typically used as a security measure to ensure that a certain level of consensus is reached before any action is taken on the blockchain. In a multisig voting system, a group of users, known as signers, are required to sign off on a proposal before it can be implemented. This can help prevent a single person or group from making unilateral decisions and ensure that decisions are made through a more democratic process. Multisig voting is often used in the context of DAOs and other decentralized systems. Multisig voting stipulates the members who will have a private key and the minimum number of key holders needed for a transaction to be approved (Petersen *et al.*, 1995; Noizat, 2015). For example, a 7-of-10 multisig protocol would require seven out of 10 parties to sign off on a transaction before it could be executed. This means that in a DAO with 10 private keys, the proposal would require the approval of at least seven key holders in order to pass. Then seven key holders are enough to govern the DAO.

Multisig voting is usually used to manage pooled DAO funds, and it requires a certain number of members to sign off for transferring actions. The multisignature fund management solutions can prevent any DAO member from moving funds on their own. Multisig voting requires a multisignature wallet, which enables multiple owners to control their shared assets.

The main advantage of this voting scheme is its security. It provides a backup plan in case something goes wrong. It ensures that each transaction is thoroughly verified before it is completed.

---

[3] https://hackernoon.com/knowledge-extractable-voting-for-blockchain-distributed-governance-radically-new-mechanisms-ed2ca47f065f.

[4] https://www.ditcraft.io/dl/ditcraft_whitepaper.pdf.

This voting scheme is for some typical proposals, especially for fund management. It is not a general voting scheme for all types of proposals. It's often recommended for organizations that prefer advanced security and privacy. The scheme could be much faster if the multikey holders can sign efficiently. However, adding the extra signature requirements might also cause inefficiency for a transaction if the number of key holders is not quickly reached. Moreover, setting up a multisig wallet might require the members to have some basic technical knowledge. More importantly, it is also possible that the multisig key holders can collude to make decisions against the interests of the other DAO members. Gnosis Safe, Aragon Client DAOs and BitDAO (Table 4) are examples that used this voting scheme.

2.6. *Holographic consensus*

Holographic consensus is a proposed mechanism for achieving consensus in a decentralized system. The idea is that the consensus of a large number of low-power nodes can be inferred from the consensus of a smaller number of high-power nodes, similar to how the information on the boundary of a region is

Table 4. Examples for the applications of multisig voting.

Examples	Description
Gnosis Safe	Gnosis Safe is a multisig wallet that allows users to securely store and manage their cryptocurrency assets. It is built on the Ethereum blockchain and utilizes smart contract technology to provide users with a user-friendly and secure way to manage their digital assets. The Gnosis Safe uses a multisig voting system, which means that multiple signatures are required to authorize a transaction. This is designed to provide an additional layer of security and prevent unauthorized access to user funds. Additionally, Gnosis Safe also provides users with a range of advanced features, such as support for ERC-20 and ERC-721 tokens, a customizable user interface, and integration with decentralized applications (dApps).
Aragon Client	Aragon Client is a dApp built on the Ethereum blockchain that allows users to create and manage DAOs. It provides a user-friendly interface for creating and customizing DAOs, as well as tools for managing and voting on proposals within the organization. The Aragon Client is built on the Aragon Network, a platform for building decentralized organizations that aims to make it easy for anyone to create and manage a DAO. The Aragon Client is an open-source project and is governed by the Aragon Association, a non-profit organization that oversees the development and maintenance of the Aragon Network.
BitDAO	BitDAO supports builders of the decentralized economy. It is an open platform for proposals that are voted upon by BIT token holders, and is agnostic to chains and projects.

equivalent to the information inside the region.[5] The mechanism is also a variant of futarchy, which is based on the notion that the market participants are more efficient and smarter than the elected voters at predicting outcomes.[6] This allows for more efficient and scalable consensus compared to traditional methods. Holographic consensus is a governance mechanism initiated by DAOstack.

By staking their tokens, users can influence the direction and governance of the DAO, and may also be eligible for rewards or other benefits. The exact mechanics of staking in a DAO can vary depending on the specific organization, but generally involve holding and locking up a certain amount of tokens for a certain period of time in order to participate in the DAO's governance.

Any user who satisfies reputation requirements could submit the proposals. But only the proposals with enough attention are more likely to be reviewed and voted. According to the voting mechanism, small groups will make decisions on behalf of the majority. An incentive is provided to align the interest between the voting group and the majority. However, DAOs are large organizations, and many proposals could be submitted. DAOstack brings in a cryptocurrency called GEN to select the proposal with the most potential for the voting group.

GEN can be used as a stake for or against a proposal. It is like a bet on the submitted proposals. The proposal with most GEN will catch the collective attention of the voters. If anyone stakes for the proposal and the proposal is passed, he/she can be awarded more GENs. However, if the proposal fails, the betting GEN will be taken. Therefore, in order to bet on the right proposal, the GEN stakers will investigate each proposal and make sure they bet on the most potential one. Thus, the one with the highest attention could be more likely to benefit the future of the DAO.

The GEN token is to tap the incentive structure for improving DAOstack ecosystem. Using GEN enables both stakers and voters to be in the same ecosystem, so they have the same interest in making DAOstack more useful and making GEN more valuable. Using other cryptocurrencies like Ether might deviate the purpose to other uses.

---

[5] Holographic principle states that the information on the boundary of a region is equivalent to the information inside the region. Imagine a holographic image, the information that creates the image is encoded on the boundary of the holographic film, this information is equivalent to the information of the whole image that is inside the film. In the context of consensus, the idea is that the consensus of a large number of low-power nodes in a decentralized system can be inferred from the consensus of a smaller number of high-power nodes. Just as the information on the boundary of a holographic film is equivalent to the information inside the film, the consensus of a small group of high-power nodes is equivalent to the consensus of the entire network of low-power nodes.

[6] https://blog.ethereum.org/2014/08/21/introduction-futarchy.

The staking system enables anyone with GEN to predict and choose most DAO-aligned proposals, so the proposal with top attention is more likely to be passed. The passing requirements could be dynamic according to the staking system. The proposal with high potential could be passed quickly with fewer votes than other proposals. Thus, a smaller group of voters could effectively vote for the whole voter group and make quick decisions with value alignment.

Holographic consensus has some potential benefits. For example, it can potentially scale to very large, decentralized organizations, as it allows for stakeholders to participate in decision-making without requiring a direct vote on every issue; it provides a transparent and auditable way for stakeholders to track decision-making in decentralized organizations. By allowing stakeholders to view the voting history and results, as well as the reasoning and arguments behind decisions, it can help to build trust and promote more accountable governance. Moreover, it can potentially increase voter engagement and participation by allowing stakeholders to delegate their voting power to trusted third parties or to participate in specific issue-based votes. This can help to promote a more active and engaged community of stakeholders in decentralized organizations. However, there is no free lunch. The drawback of this voting scheme could be the possibility that the one with high attention and influence might be due to some hype and the one with more valuable potential might thus be neglected.

DXdao, necDAO and DAOstack are examples (Table 5) that adopted this voting scheme.

2.7. *Conviction voting*

Conviction voting is a newly developed voting scheme, which is based on both aggregated preference and time. It is designed to align the interests of token

Table 5. Examples for the applications of holographic consensus voting.

Examples	Description
Dxdao	DXdao is a DAO that operates a suite of DeFi protocols. The organization recently implemented holographic consensus voting to allow its token holders to participate in decision-making regarding the allocation of resources and the direction of the protocol.
necDAO	necDAO is built atop the DAOstack framework and uses holographic consensus through the alchemy interface.
DAOstack	DAOstack is a platform for building and managing DAOs on the Ethereum blockchain. It provides a set of tools and frameworks that enable individuals and groups to collaborate and make decisions in a decentralized and transparent manner.

Table 6. Examples for the applications of conviction voting.

Examples	**Description**
Giveth	Giveth is a community-driven platform that uses conviction voting to allocate funds and resources to various projects. With conviction voting, Giveth allows stakeholders to allocate tokens to specific projects or causes, and the allocation of funds is based on the strength of conviction of stakeholders, rather than just their token holdings.
Common Stack	Common Stack is a DAO platform that uses conviction voting to make decisions about the allocation of funds and resources. With conviction voting, stakeholders can pledge their tokens to different initiatives, and the allocation of funds is based on the strength of conviction of each stakeholder.
MetaCartel	MetaCartel is a DAO platform that uses conviction voting to make decisions about the allocation of funds and resources to various projects. With conviction voting, stakeholders can pledge their tokens to specific initiatives, and the allocation of funds is based on the strength of conviction of each stakeholder.

holders with the long-term success of the organization. In a conviction voting system, members of the community can vote on proposals by staking their tokens for a certain period of time. The longer the stake period, the more "conviction" a member has in their vote and the more weight their vote carries. This system is designed to incentivize community members to think carefully about the long-term implications of their vote and to discourage short-term thinking and speculation. By staking their tokens for a longer period of time, members signal that they are more confident in the proposal and that they believe it will be beneficial for the organization in the long run. Table 6 shows several examples which apply the conviction voting scheme in their design.

2.8. *Rage quitting voting*

Rage quitting is a term used to describe a phenomenon that can occur in DAOs and other decentralized communities that use token-weighted voting systems. It refers to the scenario where a token holder, who is unhappy with the outcome of a vote or the direction of the organization, decides to withdraw their stake and sell their tokens, rather than continuing to support the organization. This can have a negative impact on the organization, as it can lead to a decrease in the value of the token, and it can also lead to a lack of participation in future votes.

Quitting voting is initiated by Moloch DAO and is well accepted by many DAOs using the DAOhaus platform. In a Moloch DAO, membership should be approved and permissioned by the existing full-share members. Upon approval, each member can hold either full shares or loot shares. The difference between these two shares is that the full share has both voting rights and "Ragequit" rights, while the loot share only has "Ragequit" rights. The "Ragequit" refers to a quitting mechanism for each member. The members can quit a DAO and redeem their shares in the grace period after the approval of the proposal if the approval does not align with their interests.

Proposals could be submitted by anybody (including non-members). However, they should be supported by at least one member for proceeding to the voting process. The voting process is simply collecting "agree" or "disagree" votes from the members and passing if the "agree" is more than "disagree". It does not have a quorum requirement. In some DAOs with such a voting scheme, the vote is by default considered as "agree" if the member does not vote for "disagree". When the proposal is passed, there will be a grace period. Those who voted "disagree" can withdraw their shares before the proposal's implementation. This is the "Ragequit" design so that some minor members are allowed to escape before an unwanted proposal that might represent the majority's tyranny. For example, suppose the majority members (say, 70%) would like to pass a proposal which benefits themselves (by exploiting the benefits of the rest 30% minority). In that case, the minority can protect their treasury with the "Ragequit" mechanism.

The advantages of the mechanism are sound. For example, it is a secure system against Sybil attacks as the voting is done within a permissioned group, and members are protected. It scales trustless coordination with more stakeholders than other voting mechanisms like multisig.

The downside is that the mechanism takes time to approve any proposal, given that there is a grace period. If the proposal is in urgent need, this might not be efficient. To address this concern, Moloch DAO also introduces Minion as a supplement. Minions need a quorum, that there are sufficient "Agree votes" and no "Disagree" votes, to allow early execution on proposals without "Ragequit" and the grace period. However, this modification changes the security properties of a DAO's funds, especially when the stakes in the proposal are high enough. There is a trade-off between security and efficiency. To avoid rage quitting voting, organizations can implement different measures like reducing the token liquidation speed, or making it difficult to withdraw the stake, making sure that the token holder has to wait a certain period of time before they can withdraw the stake.

MetaCartel Ventures, MolochDAO and DAOhaus[7] are experimenting with this voting scheme (Table 7).

[7] https://daohaus.mirror.xyz/U_JQtheSzdpRFqQwf9Ow3LgLNG0WMZ6ibAyrjWDu_fc.

Table 7. Examples for the applications of rage quitting voting.

Examples	Description
MolochDAO	MolochDAO is a collective that funds Ethereum-based projects. In MolochDAO, members can rage quit if they disagree with a proposal that has passed by submitting a request to exit the DAO and retrieving their staked tokens.
MetaCartel	MetaCartel is a DAO that funds Ethereum-based projects. In MetaCartel, members can also rage quit if they disagree with a proposal that has passed by withdrawing their funds from the DAO.
DAOhaus	DAOhaus is a DAO that operates on the Ethereum blockchain. In a DAO, decisions are made by token holders who vote on proposals using their tokens. Anyone who contributed funds can vote with their dollars if they don't like our direction.

2.9. *Appraisal of the schemes*

We follow the literature to compare each voting system from five aspects as follows (Sampigethaya and Poovendran, 2006; Wu *et al.*, 2014; López García, 2016).

Efficiency: Speed of selecting the potential proposals and approval of urgent proposals.
Fairness: Each voter has equal rights to vote.
Scalability: Ability to adjust storage, computation, and communication needs according to the number of voters.
Robustness: The resistance to attacks or collusion.
Incentive Schemes: Whether the design motivates the behavior of participants.

The comparison in Table 8 is a relative appraisal. We can see that there is not any "perfect" scheme. There are pros and cons for all the schemes. A compromise approach is to combine some voting schemes and tries to design a better one. We propose a new scheme with prominent features from holographic consensus and conviction voting.

There could be other voting scheme concepts. For example, liquidity voting, a.k.a. proxy voting. The idea behind liquid voting is to align the interests of token holders with the interests of the DAO. By giving token holders more voting power in proportion to the number of tokens they hold, the system incentivizes them to hold onto their tokens and engage with the DAO, rather than selling them. This helps to ensure that the long-term health and success of the DAO is aligned with the interests of its token holders. Some of the voting schemes introduced in the paper could be a variant to the liquidity voting, e.g., quadratic liquidity voting is a hybrid scheme to apply the quadratic notion with a liquidity voting concept.

Table 8. Comparison of listed schemes.

	Efficiency	**Fairness**	**Scalability**	**Robustness**	**Incentive Schemes**
Token-based Quorum Voting	Medium	High	Low	Low	Not
Quadratic Voting	Medium	Low	Medium	Medium	Not
Weighted Voting and Reputation-based Voting	Medium	Low	Medium	High	Yes
KEV	Medium	Low	Medium	High	Yes
The Multisig Voting	Medium	High	Low	Low	Not
Holographic Consensus	High	High	High	Medium	Yes
Conviction Voting	Low	Medium	Medium	High	Not
Rage Quitting Voting	Low	High	Medium	Medium	Not

3. A New Voting Design Notion

This section proposes a new hypothetical voting mechanism for a purely decentralized and permissionless DAO governance. We focus on permissionless characteristics as it is more general. The design is to accelerate conviction voting with a holographic mechanism.

We first define the voting member as the stakeholder of a DAO. The DAO governance power is represented as the stakes of all the resources. If we tokenize the resources, the address with at least one token stake is considered a member. The membership is permissionless, but the interest is aligned as it might be costly to obtain the token. To avoid excess voting power from vast new members or large-stake members, the basic voting process will follow conviction voting. Therefore, time and stake are both essential for passing the proposals, the same as traditional conviction voting.

For any proposal submitted, we dynamically introduce an estimated duration of the proposal (e.g., the average duration of recent proposals). If the proposal cannot be passed within this pre-estimated duration, it will fail automatically. In other words, we introduce a veto possibility into conviction voting.

We know that the downside of the conviction voting mechanism is that it takes time to approve an urgent proposal. To address this concern, we introduce a blind betting mechanism: Each member could choose whether to bet on any proposals with a certain number of their tokens. The betting is unseen to all the betters. If there are more betting tokens of "pass" than "veto", the governance power will be accelerated, and the proposal could be approved faster. If there are more betting tokens of "veto" than the "pass", the governance power will be slowed down, and the proposal could fail faster.

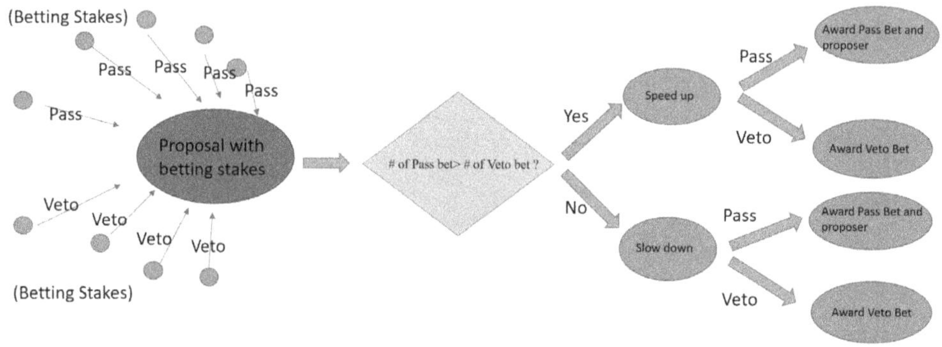

Fig. 1. Voting and rewarding process.

Incentive schemes are introduced in the betting process. If the proposal passes, the betting tokens of "veto" will be confiscated. Some of the confiscated amounts will be used to award the proposal submitter, and the rest will be distributed to the one with betting tokens of "pass" proportionally according to the bet. If the proposal fails, the "pass" betting tokens will be confiscated. However, there is no reward for the proposal submitter, and the confiscated tokens will be distributed to the one with betting tokens of "veto" proportionally according to the bet. Because it is a blind betting process, it is possible that there is only one way of betting, i.e., if all are betting "pass" or betting "veto", then no rewards will be distributed. Nevertheless, the proposal will still be accelerated or slowed down.

Under the incentive schemes, everyone is incentivized to submit a good proposal that is more likely to pass and get rewarded. More importantly, the betting process provides incentives for voters to vote carefully if they place a bet on the proposal. Urgent and good proposals could be speeded up and approved faster. It is more efficient than a pure conviction voting mechanism.

Fig. 1. illustrates the process for our proposed scheme. The proposed scheme could be easily extended to a permissioned scenario. Permissioned cases are often used in a secure database with entry controls. It has restrictions on the users and voters, but this is irrelevant to this voting scheme *per se*.

4. Conclusion

We have reviewed several prevailing voting schemes and made a comparison among the schemes. There are pros and cons to each scheme we introduced. The schemes are mainly developed and implemented by DAO service platforms (Zhao *et al.*, 2022) such as Aragon, Moloch, DAOstack, and SubDAO.[8]

[8] SubDAO is a web3 protocol that helps manage digital assets through multisig and DAO.

The development of DAO is not only targeting a static organizational future. It should keep improving the organization constantly by absorbing good designs. Our hypothetical scheme has a better design incorporating key features from other schemes. However, it is not flawless and might face challenges in implementation. Nevertheless, we aim to inspire innovative design thinking. Because all the voting schemes are applied in DAO, they have also been widely used in social governance like elections or corporate governance. The research on the voting mechanism could be important for the decision-making of public issues, and any improvement or progress could have profound inspiration for realistic governance.

Acknowledgments

ChatGPT, OpenAI assisted in some basic research and enhanced the flow of the thoughts in this paper.

References

Benaloh, J., 1987, Verifiable Secret-ballot Elections, Ph.D. Thesis, Yale University.

Boyd, C., 1990, A New Multiple Key Cipher and an Improved Voting Scheme, in *Advances in Cryptology — EUROCRYPT'89*, Springer-Verlag, pp. 617–625.

Chaum, D. L., 1981, Untraceable Electronic Mail, Return Addresses, and Digital Pseudonyms, *Communications of the ACM*, 24, 84–90, doi:10.1145/358549.358563.

Cramer, R., R. Gennaro, and B. Schoenmakers, 1997, A Secure and Optimally Efficient Multi-authority Election Scheme, in *Advances in Cryptology — EUROCRYPT'97*, Lecture Notes in Computer Science, Vol. 1233, Springer-Verlag, pp. 103–118.

El Faqir, Y., J. Arroyo, and S. Hassan, 2020, An Overview of Decentralized Autonomous Organizations on the Blockchain, in *Proceedings of the 16th International Symposium on Open Collaboration,* doi:10.1145/3412569.3412579.

Fujioka, A., T. Okamoto, and K. Ohta, 1993, A Practical Secret Voting Scheme for Large-scale Elections, in *Advances in Cryptology, AUSCRYPT'92*, Lecture Notes in Computer Science, Vol. 718, Springer, pp. 244–251.

Hassan, S., and P. De Filippi, 2021, Decentralized Autonomous Organization, *Internet Policy Review* 10(2), 1–10, https://doi.org/10.14763/2021.2.1556.

López García, D. A., 2016, A Flexible e-Voting Scheme for Debating Tools, *Computers & Security*, 56, 50–62.

Jakobsson, M., A. Juels, and R. Rivest, 2002, Making Mix Nets Robust for Electronic Voting by Randomized Partial Checking, in *Proceedings of USENIX Security'02*, USENIX Association, pp. 339–353.

Kaal, W. A., 2021, Blockchain-based Corporate Governance, *Stanford Journal of Blockchain Law & Policy* (Online), 4(1).

Morrison, R., N. C. H. L. Mazey, and S. C. Wingreen, 2020, The DAO Controversy: The Case for a New Species of Corporate Governance? *Frontiers in Blockchain* 3(25), 1–13, doi:10.3389/fbloc.2020.00025.

Neff, C. A., 2004, Practical High Certainty Intent Verification for Encrypted Votes, Citeseer.

Noizat, P.. 2015, Blockchain Electronic Vote, in *Handbook of Digital Currency*, Academic Press, pp. 453–461.

Petersen, H., P. Horster, and M. Michels, 1995, Blind Multisignature Schemes and their Relevance to Electronic Voting, in *11th Annual Computer Security Applications Conference*, IEEE Press, pp. 149–155.

Quarfoot, D., D. von Kohorn, K. Slavin, R. Sutherland, D. Goldstein, and E. Konar, Quadratic Voting in the Wild: Real People, Real Votes, *Public Choice* 172(1–2), 283–303.

Ribeiro, C., and R. Joaquim, 2012, An Efficient and Highly Sound Voter Verification Technique and Its Implementation, in *E-Voting and Identity, Third International Conference, VoteID 2012*, Springer-Verlag, pp. 104–121.

Sako, K., and J. Kilian, 1995, Receipt-free Mix-type Voting Scheme — A Practical Solution to the Implementation of a Voting Booth, in *Advances in Cryptology — EUROCRYPT '95, International Conference on the Theory and Application of Cryptographic Techniques*, Saint-Malo, France, pp. 393–403.

Sampigethaya, K., and R. Poovendran, 2006, A Framework and Taxonomy for Comparison of Electronic Voting Schemes, *Computers & Security* 25, 137–153.

Wu, Z. Y., J. C. Wu, S. C. Lin, and C. Wang, 2014, An Electronic Voting Mechanism for Fighting Bribery and Coercion, *Journal of Network and Computer Applications* 40, 139–150.

Yermack, D., 2017, Corporate Governance and Blockchains, *Review of Finance* 21(1), 7–31, doi:10.1093/rof/rfw074.

Zhao, X., P. Ai, F. Lai, X. (R.) Luo, and J. Benitez, 2022, Task Management in Decentralized Autonomous Organization, *Journal of Operations Management* 68(6–7), 649–674, https://doi.org/10.1002/joom.1179.

Zhuang, Q., Y. Liu, L. Chen, and Z. Ai, 2019, Proof of Reputation: A Reputation-based Consensus Protocol for Blockchain Based Systems, in *Proceedings of the 1st International Electronics Communication Conference (IECC'19)*, Association for Computing Machinery, New York, NY, USA, pp. 131–138, https://doi.org/10.1145/3343147.3343169.

A Commentary on "A Case Study of Ant Finance's Innovation Journey — From a Platform Economy Perspective"

Xin (Cindy) Deng

Nanyang Business School,
Nanyang Technological University, Singapore

The large populations and growing numbers of small and medium-sized enterprises in the Asia-Pacific drive the need for financial services, which has served as a catalyst for the expansion of FinTech in this region. It is worth noting that Alibaba and Tencent had risen to the top ten global technology companies by market capitalization prior to the COVID-19 pandemic. This establishes China as a leader in FinTech in the Asia-Pacific with the rapid development of numerous FinTech segments such as digital payment, consumer finance, microlending, InsurTech, and WealthTech. The paper "A Case Study of Ant Finance's Innovation Journey — From a Platform Economy Perspective" provides an in-depth discussion on Ant Group, the FinTech arm of Alibaba, which covers nearly every segment of FinTech services. It illustrates how platform economy developed in a country with the second-largest population.

The paper starts the discussion with the suspension of Ant Group's IPO. However, the regulatory crackdown is unsurprising. It can be attributed to two primary reasons. First, the inherent "winner-takes-all" nature of the FinTech industry leads to a concentration of market power and resources. According to statistics from the China Financial Technology Enterprise Database, the number of new financial technology companies registered grew from 351 to 5,122 from 2008 to 2014. The growth rate between 2013 and 2014 was over 100%. Then, the market began to integrate. The number of newly registered FinTech companies substantially declined. Only 432 new financial technology companies were established by 2017, which is only 8% of the number from 2014. Large platforms have the capability to leverage vast user bases, rich business data, and advanced technological infrastructure. Moreover, these dominant entities once imposed conditions like exclusive agreements on capital seekers, distorting competition and potentially leading to an inefficient allocation of financial resources. These phenomena naturally invite regulatory scrutiny.

Second, Chinese regulators have long considered financial security and stability crucial to achieving economic development. The 2022 Central Economic Work Conference also stressed the need to prevent and resolve financial risks to avoid regional and systemic risks. However, new risks emerge with FinTech's rapid expansion. For example, advanced technologies like big data, biometric identification, and deep learning can exploit these data breaches for serious crimes such as financial theft or other illegal activities. Furthermore, the complexity of FinTech provides a cover for misuse. It can be challenging for regulators to promptly and accurately detect financial crimes facilitated by technology. If these new risks are not adequately addressed and intertwined with other financial risks, they could lead to systemic risks, endangering the stability of China's financial and economic system.

As this discussion is based on platform economy literature, it might be worth incorporating several recent papers that discuss the tokenization of platforms. There is growing tension between digital platforms and their users; as digital platforms such as Amazon, Google, and Facebook become increasingly pervasive in our daily lives, their large networks of users facilitate not only monopoly power in pricing but also extensive access to users' private data. Given that network effects are essential for the success of online platforms, platforms typically invest substantial resources to subsidize user participation to build a large user base. The equity holders of these platforms bear the costs of subsidizing user participation to maximize future advertising revenue, which scales with the user base. Tokenization protects users by shifting ownership and control of the platform from initial equity holders to users; but this shift potentially eliminates any incentivized owner who might subsidize user engagement to enhance network effects. The model presented by Sockin and Xiong (2023) highlights the trade-off induced by decentralization between safeguarding users and subsidizing their participation in the presence of network effects.

Furthermore, Goldstein *et al.* (2023) show how utility tokens can curb the rent-seeking behavior of powerful two-sided platforms while still capturing efficiency gains from network effects. Their model conceptualizes platforms where buyers and sellers transact using tokens, which are the sole currency and can be traded on secondary markets. Tokenization commits a platform to forgo monopolistic rents that come with platform control, leading to competitively sustainable prices in the long run. They also discuss how the potential entry of new competitors can motivate developers to tokenize their platforms and outline scenarios where regulatory intervention might be necessary to ensure tokenization.

Overall, as platform economies continue to evolve, the interplay between market forces and regulatory frameworks will undoubtedly remain a critical area of scholarly and practical interest.

References

Sockin, M. and Xiong, W. (2023), Decentralization through tokenization. *The Journal of Finance*, 78: 247–299. https://doi.org/10.1111/jofi.13192.

Goldstein, I., Gupta D., and Sverchkov R., Utility tokens as a commitment to competition. *The Journal of Finance* (forthcoming).

A Case Study of Ant Finance's Innovation Journey — From a Platform Economy Perspective*

Herve Alexandre[†,§] and Kok Lian Woo[‡,||]

[†]*Université Paris Dauphine — PSL, Place du Maréchal de Lattre deTassigny 75016 Paris Cedex 16, France*

[‡]*Shenzhen Technology University, 3002 Lantian Road Pingshan, Shenzhen, Guangdong 518118, P. R. China*

[§]*herve.alexandre@dauphine.psl.eu*

[||]*jackwoo@sztu.edu.cn*

During the spring of 2021, the Chinese government profoundly changed its relationship with large digital platforms; the government had decided to strengthen their supervision, fight against monopolies, and promote fair competition. Until then, technology giants such as Alibaba, Tencent, Baidu, and JD.Com dominated a fast-growing market, especially in China, where Fintech represented a very important part of the retail market among middle-class consumers. Various political and economic reasons can be provided for this choice. This paper showcases the economic power of the two-sided markets approach of these platforms today and describes the late but violent reaction of the Chinese government, worried about its economic and monetary sovereignty.

Keywords: Innovation; Ant Finance; platform economy; China.

*This Chapter was originally published in the *World Scientific Annual Review of Fintech*, Vol. 1, No. 1, doi: 10.1142/S2811004823500057.

[§]Corresponding author.

1. Introduction

On November 3, 2020, the world's supposedly largest IPO to raise $34.4 billion from dual listings in Shanghai and Hong Kong was halted by Chinese regulators, two days before the public offering. Chinese regulators reasoned that "major issues" and "failure to meet information requirements" were found in the proposed listing and ordered an indefinite suspension. The disappearance of the founder of the group, Jack Ma, fueled speculations regarding his possible arrest. Speculations also stated that the IPO pullback was the government's revenge on Ma's open criticism of the Chinese banking system in front of the regulators. Statements implied that there was "lip service" from the regulators in resolving the SME financing issues, which led to a mismatched allocation of capital in the country. Chinese banks were criticized as "pawnshops", which only gave loans to companies that did not need money, and therefore, many unfinanced companies turned insolvent.

The abrupt halt of Ant Finance's IPO had raised regulatory and public deliberations over the roles of the gigantic data controllers and possible measures to ensure fair competition. Alipay and WeChatPay accounted for 55.4% and 38.8% of the mobile payment market in China, respectively (iResearch, 2020). Alibaba's e-commerce platform Ant Financial (referred to as "Ant" hereafter) had access to social, behavioral, and transaction data of over 700 million consumers and 80 million merchants. According to Ant's prospectus, microlending revenues in the first half of 2020 amounted to approximately RMB 28.6 billion ($4.4 billion) which accounted for nearly 40% of its operating revenue. Moreover, 98% of the lending was funded by domestic provincial banks and not recorded on Ant's balance sheet. The loan facilitation allowed Ant to operate on low capital for high profit, while the interest, credit, and market risks remained within the traditional banking system. Banks used Ant's platform to expand their credit businesses and used Ant's consumer data and cloud resources for a fee.

Ant coordinated the credit supply from traditional banks and matched it with the financing demand from its microlending customers. Ant operated on a model that took advantage of information asymmetries in the market. Besides facilitating financial product trading over its platform, Ant also had investments and subsidiaries that provide financial services directly to its consumer platform using different banking licenses. For example, MyBank had a banking license to provide digital online banking services to SMEs in China, and underwrote loans enabled through Ant's CreditTech platforms. Ant also ran consumer deposit accounts, financing products, and money market funds (MMFs) in its own name and capacity. Similar to a financial institution, Ant performed a financial intermediary role in the capital allocation process. Questions were raised against Ant's monopolistic powers, and several regulatory crackdowns were targeted against platform operators in China, including Alibaba, Tencent, and DiDi; these companies were all listed on the US Stock Exchange. Regulatory actions included fines, penalties, business suspensions, rectification orders, preventing new users from enlisting, and off-boarding from Chinese App stores. At that time, big tech firms' platforms had spread widely across many subsidiaries and industries, cutting across different regulators' remits. This created challenges in the supervisory framework. What was Ant's platform economy model? How did Ant coordinate various network activities and externalities and how could regulators manage a platform's monopolistic influence but remain pro-innovative?

An in-depth case study on Ant's business from a platform economy theory perspective can help scholars understand the platform evolutionary process, help policymakers evaluate the role of a firm in the ecosystem, and help enact appropriate policies to govern financial risks. The structure of this paper begins with a literature review of the platform economy and China's financial system. This is followed by a discussion of the case study research methodology. It continues with a review of Ant's platform network and the evolution of economies. It then discusses the research questions from a platform economy perspective, considering the uniqueness of China's financial system. It also provides a theoretical model that explains Ant's platform economy and discusses its potential for generalization. Finally, it concludes with some limitations identified in this research, and that further studies are needed to generalize the theoretical model.

2. Theoretical Background on Platform Economy

How a platform operates and generates rent to its operator through multisided markets is the central question of this study. The economic study of platforms is largely based on an analysis of network externalities (Farrell and Saloner, 1985; Katz and Shapiro, 1994) and pricing in two-sided markets (Evans, 2003; Rochet and Tirole, 2003; Trabucchi and Buganza, 2021). In the work on network economics, Katz and Shapiro (1985) found that in certain situations, consumption of certain goods and services will only be meaningful when others (counterparties) also use the same goods and services. For example, a telecommunication system requires a sender to deliver and a receiver to receive a message to create value from its usage. Katz and Shapiro (1994) also pointed out that it is important to look at the value produced from the combined consumption of goods and services in the value chain and from the entire ecosystem. For example, Apple began to embrace the concept of ecosystems and two-sided markets with the opening of the App Store in July 2008. The App Store initially had 500 applications on it at launch. It quickly grew with the increasing popularity of its underlying operating system IOS amongst software developers. By 2017, it featured over 2.1 million applications. Therefore, it is important to note that systems and the economics of an ecosystem should be analyzed holistically, instead of only investigating the product, when formulating strategies for the pricing, market structure, value proposition, network, and network externalities in a platform economy.

In the study of systems and the network approach, Katz and Shapiro (1994, 1985) further pointed to three key variables: expectations, coordination, and compatibility. Expectations refer to a system's capacity to attract new players and increase their participation. It is essential that the evolution of one part of the system is coordinated with the evolution of the other components. Lastly, compatibility creates a mechanism for the interplay and interconnectivity of a product and a service in the ecosystem. In doing so, it can foster creativity and eventually increase participation in the network and also network externalities, in terms of the numbers of producers, traders, operators, users, and complementary services and products offered. To create and sustain a platform economy, it is necessary to develop a critical mass of users, coordinate network actors and their activities, and finally establish a compatibility standard for services and products, as analyzed by Farrell and Saloner (1985).

The two-sided market (Armstrong, 2006; Rochet and Tirole, 2003, 2006) focuses on prices and the structure of tariffs by creating an intermediary that connects different user groups to satisfy their needs. For example, the Apple Store connects consumers, to search, buy, and install apps on their smartphones, with app developers, to promote and sell their products. The more consumer groups and participants there are in the network, the higher the attractiveness and sustainability of the platform. According to Evans (2003), a market would be viable and increase collective welfare if there are two or more different consumer groups, positive externalities that arise when different consumers are connected, and, finally, an intermediary enabling the expectations of the various consumer groups to be met. For example, ride hailing (Uber) and e-commerce (Amazon) platforms are successful because of their large numbers of users and consumer groups who participate in the supply, logistics, consumption, and payment of goods and services, which enables the fulfillment of the benefits to participants. The price structure depends on the attractiveness, numbers of participants and profiles, and accessibility of the platform. The operating costs of the platform can be subsidized by an externality (such as an advertiser), a regulator (such as municipal government), a product or service producer, a consumer, and/or a combination of these (Armstrong, 2006; Eisenmann *et al.*, 2006; Rochet and Tirole, 2003).

The sustainability of a platform is a function of the operator's ability to influence innovation, standardize adoption, and make future choices (Gawer and Cusumano, 2014). A leader's dominant position can make it possible to define the market operating rules, maintain a significant market share, and continue to be profitable (Boudreau and Hagiu, 2009). The winner-takes-all position is so strong that it justifies large investments in emerging segments. However, in the case of digital platforms, it is important not to overlook the considerable difficulty in retaining customers. A competitor is only one click away, and it is very easy for a participant on one side of a two-sided market to change platform. Competition is intense, and the maintenance of established positions can be challenging (Ferrier *et al.*, 1999; Tiwana *et al.*, 2010; Cennamo and Santalo, 2013). Nothing prevents a participant from being present on several platforms simultaneously, and to switch between platforms. The only thing the platform operator can do is make it harder for users to switch to the competitors' platform by creating inconveniences and imposing costs for changing.

Smartphone-enabled platforms allow owners to capture a significant share of the value chain at the expense of partners, who may be the main innovation creators. It also dramatically increases the number of participants in the network and allows the proliferation of multisided markets. The potential for the emergence of direct and indirect externalities is also much greater. As a result, it is more difficult for platform owners to exercise control (Parker and Van Alstyne, 2018) and to manage the trade-off between innovativeness and size (Panico and Cennamo, 2022). The current literature on the subject of platform economy has largely focused on network and two-sided market theories. For example, Pon *et al.* (2014) highlighted the open access features in the Android platform and Nucciarelli *et al.* (2017) discussed the effect of crowdfunding platforms.

Platform economy proliferation has further expanded the boundary of a firm through its dynamic network and self-growing externalities. Market concentration risk increases because of new barriers to entry based on network effects, economies of scale, and strong competitive value of data. A large platform economy also creates systemic risks, cybersecurity, and personal data privacy issues. Regulators are challenged by "too big to fail" or "winner take all" phenomenon in the platform economy. Some platform operators are direct providers of financial services, and some are enablers for platform users to interact and consume financial services themselves. The higher the complexity, nature, and volume of transactions, the more the interdependencies between the platform operator and network externalities. But, the higher the functional equivalence is between incumbents and new entrants, the lower the need to formulate new rules and develop new supervision practices becomes (de las Heras Ballell, 2020).

3. Methodology

Our paper aims to explain why and how a phenomenon is developed in a certain way. The case study research approach is recommended for situations where the focus is on providing explanations for a contemporary issue or an understudied phenomenon (Yin, 1994). Nevertheless, due to the complexity of real-world situations and the interconnectivity of different rivals, providing a true and accurate explanation of a research phenomenon using the explanatory case study approach is difficult and complicated, as the researcher has almost no control over the described events (Yin, 1994). Explanatory research is performed to help study complex systems in the fields of business, public policy, and social science. It does not provide conclusive evidence of the causal relationship of the phenomena, but it can help us understand and explain the situation better and effectively predict the potential implications.

This study is based on a combination of primary and secondary data obtained from executive interviews, focus group discussions, business seminars, document research, government reports and statistics, researchers' observations, corporate announcements, annual reports, internal newsletters, prospectus, and data published on corporate websites. The case study design, combined with real-life events, shows that numerous sources of evidence through replication rather than sampling logic help to enhance the generalizability of the research results.

4. Ant's Platform Economy

Due to its e-commerce platform's economic scale leverage, Alibaba entered the Fintech service sector via Alipay and expanded its footprint from third-party payments to online banking, microlending, insurance, and wealth management businesses under Ant (Elia *et al.*, 2022). Alipay was established as a third-party payment offering in 2004 and has become critical to Alibaba, facilitating transactions in its e-commerce and microlending businesses. During a period of high competition between American and Chinese digital platforms in China (Li, 2021; Zeng and Glaister, 2016), Chinese platforms such as Ant progressively gained a huge and definitive advantage (Huang *et al.*, 2015). Ant was established as a small microfinance service group in 2014. It focused on serving small- and micro-enterprises as well as individual consumers by providing inclusive financial services through platform economy and technology. An Ant officer said, "We insist on 'small deposit and small lending' approach (mainly to provide consumer financing of less than RMB 200,000 and SME loans not exceeding RMB 5 million) to diversify risk and penetrate the niche market by levering on our established networks and platform economies in Alibaba."

Ant's platform economy development can be divided into three phases: platform incubation (2004–2013), platform expansion (2014–2015), and platform regionalization (2016–now). Platform incubation began with Alipay as an online payment offering for Alibaba's e-commerce businesses. Alipay solved the trust issue in online transactions by withholding payment to the seller until receiving confirmation of goods or services acceptance from the buyer. Alipay earned processing fees from the seller to act as an intermediary. Alipay began to accumulate short-term (mostly 7–10 days) deposits and small amounts of funds from a large base of buyers through its intermediary accounts, without paying any interest to the depositors. This was an early form of interest-free money market fund. It was a two-sided market with online merchants on one side and buyers on the other side, while the platform served as the transaction and fund transfer intermediary. To accelerate its platform expansion, it began to offer mobile payment services (Alipay Wallet) to merchants and users outside the Alibaba e-commerce network. Ant played an expanded role as a network coordinator to maintain the operation, risk, and data governance of the platform. It also took advantage of collecting data from various forms of transactions and used these transaction data to innovate and develop new functionality.

In 2016, Ant started to offer its Fintech solutions externally, to financial institutions domestically and to partners in the Asian market through investment and technology collaboration, e.g. with India's Paytm in 2015, Thailand's Ascend Money in 2016, Korea's Kakao Pay, the Philippines' Mynt, Singapore's HelloPay, Indonesia's Dana, and Malaysia's e-wallet, to name a few. Ant did not simply replicate China's operating model in these markets; instead, it sought collaboration with local market players who had deep knowledge of domestic regulations, user behaviors, and market norms. Ant played the role of a network constructor to develop a multilayered, scalable, and adaptable ecosystem based on an open platform model, becoming a type of meta-organization (Kretschmer *et al.*, 2022).

Platform development success at Ant can be attributed to network effects. Alipay started as an escrow service for Alibaba's marketplace. In economic terms, Ant reduced the transaction costs for its users. Services were easier to access in real-time at no or low costs compared to the traditional financial service providers. For example, the cost to perform know-your-customer (KYC) checks on a client was so much cheaper due to automation on the platform, than when performed by a bank. This in turn enabled granting credit to small customers, a client segment unattractive to the banks. To create strong network effects, a platform needed to achieve high user engagement and rich user experiences. Ant rapidly assembled novel capabilities to satisfy customer needs in their network, ranging from lifestyle, financing, investment, and insurance to the international fund transfer products. Alipay was central to the platform and continues to build and integrate new capabilities to meet the increasing demands of the network's user groups. By leveraging its capabilities to capture, process, and learn from big data of various sources in the network, Ant was able to identify service gaps, create more personalized services, manage and detect risks in real-time, and predict and meet unfulfilled financial service demands through partnerships with financial institutions. As the platform evolved, it rapidly assembled new capabilities by expanding the functionalities and externalities in the network. It connected consumers, merchants, financial institutions, and asset managers through a platform economy and redefined rent allocation among the network actors. It also offered local and cross-border banking and fund transfer services to banks and technology companies.

As pointed out by Katz and Shapiro (1994, 1985), an increase in the number of participants in a network allows the proliferation of multisided markets and improves the potential for the emergence of direct and indirect externalities. In this case, the platform owner could exercise greater control over the platform's "rules of the game" and attain a certain degree of power in determining the transaction costs and pricing on the platform. Meanwhile, financial data and financial services were required by lenders to price credit risk appropriately and provide suitable products to investors. Therefore, there was a need for partnerships and co-creation with financial institutions, not only for funding, but also for financial knowledge transfer, along with the ability to respond quickly and effectively to adjust business activities and controls in response to regulatory changes. Ant aimed to build an open financial platform economy that would bring various forms of financial services to an online digital marketplace. However, Ant needed to be careful as this strategy could also create competition (Zhu, 2019).

Ant's digital payment business generated revenue from two sources. First, it charged service fees to merchants and consumers when they transferred between Alipay and their bank accounts. Second, Ant charged handling fees from merchants who used Alipay to receive payments whether through websites, mobile apps, or QR codes. Chinese consumers preferred to use mobile payments, as they were cheaper, convenient, and popular. Many users were unbanked or under-banked. In August 2017, the People's Bank of China (PBOC), the central bank, ordered that all electronic payments needed to go through a new central bank payment clearance platform, and daily limits were set on mobile payment transactions and fund transfers. Despite these controls and limitations, Alipay continued to extend its coverage in diverse use-cases, including shopping, lifestyle, travel, transportation, finance, education, leisure, food and beverage, healthcare, public welfare, business, utility, and government agency administrative services.

5. Discussion

Both Alibaba and Ant operated on a third-party platform economy model. They did not produce or keep any stock, did not engage in direct sales and trading, and did not compete with their merchants or customers — in essence, they were a brokerage business. They created a multisided market to connect, govern, and facilitate the transaction and payment processes between platform users and network actors, to encourage network activities and the expansion of annual active users. They did not charge listing fees, but instead generated most of their revenues from advertisement and payment processing fees received from merchants. The platform model was not capital-intensive but required continued investment in IT infrastructure to keep up with data processing demands, and continuous exploration of new use-cases (R&D) to sustain its market traction. To create and sustain a platform economy, it was necessary to develop a critical mass of users, coordinate network actors and their activities, and finally create a compatibility standard for the service and product to facilitate trade on the platform (Farrell and Saloner, 1985).

Alipay was originally created to facilitate online payments and to solve e-commerce trust-related issues. Leveraging on its e-commerce platform market size and Alipay's mass usage influence, Alibaba and Ant continued to attract new players and increase their participation in the network. The evolution of the network was fueled by SME financing and the financial inclusion needs in China. The supportive approach and publication of financial innovation guidelines by the authorities from 2010 to 2020 also created a fertile ground for Ant's financial platform economy model. The QR code payment method had become a compatibility standard for mobile payments, rapidly replacing cash and bank card payments in China. By obtaining relevant banking licenses, and by moving funds across domains and engaging in deposit, asset securitization, and lending activities, Ant also created a mechanism interconnecting financial institutions and services in the platform economy. As a result, an increasing number of banks, asset managers, insurers, and financial institutions began to join in and offered their services on and around Ant's network to offload some of their activities from their balance sheet.

Alipay was the door opener for Alibaba into offering other financial services, such as the money market fund and the Wealth Management Product (WMP). In 2013, Alibaba and TianHong Asset Management co-founded Yu'E Bao (an online MMF investing in interbank loans as well as government and corporate bonds). The offering evolved from a simple excess cash account product for Alibaba's online shoppers to an e-wallet that generated returns to the account owner depending on the amount, period, and WMP invested. Consumer credit data from Alibaba's e-commerce platform were critical to Ant's financial platform operating model. Through its proprietary credit risk model, Ant could provide convenient financing solutions (up to CNY 3 million) in a couple of seconds without the need for collateral or further document review. Ant created closed-loop capital flows on its platform economy. Consumers used Alipay to carry out transactions on the e-commerce platform. Users could transfer excess cash in their Alipay account to Yu'E Bao MMF or purchase the WMP in "Ant Fortune" for additional returns. Yu'E Bao helped create a new two-sided market between various depositors and asset management firms. It allowed small individual investors to participate in money market with very low investment threshold and criteria (Armstrong, 2006; Rochet and Tirole, 2003, 2006). Pricing structure and fees of a platform depend on the attractiveness, number of participants and their profiles, and accessibility (Armstrong, 2006; Eisenmann *et al.*, 2006; Rochet and Tirole, 2003). In this case, Alibaba and Ant only charged marketing fees to the seller of financial services and individuals who need to transfer funds between Alipay and their bank accounts.

In June 2021, Ant was asked to form a commercial finance unit (the "Unit") with a capital base of $1.3 billion (RMB 8 billion). This was to limit Ant's ability to lend, on its own or in partnership with banks. Ant would only be allowed to lend to individuals, using funds generated from their own bonds and borrowed from domestic financial institutions. Ant would need to transfer its lending operations and outstanding loans to the new unit within a year. The unit would need to provide 30% of the funding for all co-loans, capped at 10 times the leverage of its registered capital. The regulator also imposed restrictions on banks and financial institutions working with online microlenders, capping the amount of joint lending with platforms. Ant's financial platform economy operation was interrupted by a regulatory crackdown. The sustainability of Ant's financial platform was determined by its ability to create a closed ecosystem (Gawer and Cusumano, 2014) and now, importantly, alignment to regulations. Alibaba's and Ant's dominant and influential position has previously allowed them to define the platform operating rules (in early 2021, Alibaba was fined $2.8 billion for violating antitrust laws), maintain a significant market share in e-commerce and digital finance, and continue to operate profitably by exploring market and regulatory gaps (Boudreau and Hagiu, 2009).

Essentially, Ant had connected to the entire financial service industry through its platform economy. However, until then, Ant was not included in the Systemically Important Financial Institution (SIFI) watch list. Regulators were concerned about the potential financial crisis and instability issues resulting from Ant's monopoly in digital payments, consumer financing, personal private data risks, and strong links to financial institutions. Ant's IPO halt was not surprising, although the timing was. To curb the potential social instability from high overdue payment interests of non-performing loans, Chinese authorities implemented a regulation to cap interest charges at a ceiling of 15.4% annual effective rate for all peer-to-peer (P2P) lending and microlending business operators. Licensed banks were not subject to such restrictions as their credit businesses (credit cards, short-term loans, and farmers' credit) were generally supported by credit or income vetting and state policies. Finally, with the rectification plan in place, it appeared that Ant would continue providing financial services using technology, but would have to change how it was organized and accounted for to meet the supervisory demands.

Ant accounted for more than half of the third-party payments market in China. By this measure, Alipay was at the threshold of being classified as a dominant player according to the regulator's definition. To avoid unfair competition, Ant needed to ensure that all its subsidiaries and controlling investments engaging in financial activities were organized as part of its financial holding company. This would mean it had to accept supervision, improve risk isolation measures, and manage related-party transactions at arm's length. Ant was requested to implement prudential supervision, improve corporate governance, standardize financial activities, and actively control high leverage and risk contagion. The liquidity risk of important fund products, such as Yu'E Bao, needed to be controlled and its balance-sheet size needed to be reduced. In short, regulating Ant as a financial holding company or a group of financial service companies was the first step that put it under supervision to provide fair competitive conditions in the market where banks were also hunting for business. Therefore, we can ask what drove the aggressive leverage at Ant to boost their financial performance before IPO? According to Ant's IPO prospectus, around 16,000-plus employees were granted restricted stock options known as Share Economic Rights (SERs), representing about 40% of the total company shares before floating. The share-based compensation scheme created pressures on management to float the company.

Regulators were also concerned with Ant's monopoly on payment data, providing an unfair advantage over their rivals. This monopoly also highlighted issues surrounding personal data privacy. To call for fair competitive behavior in the payments industry, Ant was asked to keep the credit and payment businesses separate and to stop cross-selling between the two units. It needed to eliminate links between Alipay and other financial products to safely give consumers more choices in payment methods. To break the data monopoly, Ant was requested to implement the requirements of the "Credit Reporting Industry Management Regulations", operate personal credit reporting services with a license in accordance with the law, and to collect and use personal information in accordance with the principle of "lawfulness, minimum, and necessity" to ensure personal and national information security. In the fall of 2020, Chinese regulators issued personal privacy protection regulations and IT security laws to prevent excesses and misuse of data by technology firms involved in platform expansion activities. A product manager from Ant said during our interview, "Most of us are trained in Internet application and platform development. None of us has formal financial or banking system training. As such, we need to expand our knowledge base to go deep into various types of financial products. We need to 'walk out' from our IT comfort zone and 'walk in' to the financial industry to understand the fundamental of financial systems and product development...the boundaries and grey areas. In short, we need to learn and develop our knowledge base in banking operations, regulatory requirements, and new models in Internet finance."

6. Theoretical Contribution

This study advances our understanding on the subject of platform economy by exploring the influence of owner, market, and regulatory powers on network effects and ecosystem establishments in a large digital financial service platform. We offer two contributions to the platform economy theories based on Ant's case analysis.

First, our study elucidates the role of different externalities in how a platform evolves from two-sided to multisided, and eventually to a multieconomy operating model. By using primary, qualitative data (e.g. gathering perspectives from firm management, regulators, and industry experts), we develop a three-stage platform development framework to provide deeper and more nuanced understanding into network and ecosystem evolution in a platform business model post-establishment. This framework contributes to the important research area of how a platform evolves and expands its externalities (Armstrong, 2006; Rochet and Tirole, 2003, 2006), with a particular focus on multisided digital platforms (Parker and Van Alstyne, 2018). Previous literature focuses on the influence of network owners, customers, and suppliers, yet these are common in most digital platforms. The Ant case study provides additional insights into the influence of the monopoly powers of a platform owner (Boudreau and Hagiu, 2009), regulators' legal powers (de las Heras Ballell, 2020), and consumers' social powers (Evans, 2003) in the network evolution process. Our research provides a more nuanced, empirical explanation of how a platform player expands its network and ecosystem. As the platform evolves, it rapidly assembles new capabilities by expanding the functionalities and externalities in the network. In case of a Fintech platform, it connects consumers, merchants, financial institutions, and asset managers through its platform economy and redefines the rent allocation among the network externalities. Eventually, the network goes "live" and evolves through continued learning from user and transaction data.

As a second contribution, we extended the discussion of network growth paths (Gawer and Cusumano, 2014). Although externalities represent an important factor for network growth (Boudreau and Hagiu, 2009), the institutional logic of the platform operator (Ferrier *et al.*, 1999; Tiwana *et al.*, 2010) can lead to a different growth path. For example, Ant leveraged a "financial intermediary model" repackaging its consumer loans and passing them on to traditional provincial banks for refinancing. This loan securitization process allowed Ant to offload items from its balance sheet and reduce compliance responsibilities while providing a risk-free arbitrage profit. The risk of non-performance loans was transferred to the traditional banks. As most of the consumer financing was non-secured and had high interest costs, the actual non-performing loan rate was probably higher than what was reported by Ant (and underestimated by the actual lenders — the banks). An additional finding from our study is that the platform monopoly is a double-sided sword. While monopolies create economies of scale, enhanced services, and promote innovation, the platform's market power and social influence can endanger the broader economy, financial markets, and social stability in a jurisdiction. Our research provides additional understanding to policymakers on the network effects of a monopolized platform.

7. Research Limitations

We recognize that our study portrays a stratified illustration of the platform development model rather than providing generalizable insights. The focus of our research question was to shed light on Ant's platform economy model and how it developed and was maintained. We acknowledge the limitations of our research design. First, we only consider the most active dominant externalities (e.g. financial institutions, consumers, and regulators), even when different combinations or configurations of other externalities (e.g. platform infrastructure and technology partners) were represented in the qualitative data collected. We also learn that the platform business model and network expansion strategy represent important determinants of network attractiveness, compatibility, and size. We also find that at the intersection of different externalities, combinations, and sequencing of various internal and external events, much potential for future research on platform operating models exists. But in our study, we do not analyze these determinants or their interactions. We also do not account for institutional culture, logic, and various dependencies within Alibaba and Ant. The institutional entrepreneur's approach to network effects and ecosystem development could have significant impacts on Ant's operating model.

8. Future Directions and Policy Implications

Platform operators are too complex to analyze all success factors at once. Hence we choose a focus area. Despite our efforts to represent holistically the network effects and ecosystem construction, we were unable to access the platform's operational data to validate some of the arguments. However, this area offers a highly interesting and relevant avenue for future research. Focusing on network effects and the ecosystem construction process at Ant provides a new perspective in the field of monopolistic digital financial platforms, which mostly focuses on the financial intermediary role of the platform. Future research can build on our findings, specifically for the analysis of networks and ecosystems across platforms in other financial service sectors in different jurisdictions. For example, how US big tech companies strategize and expand their platforms represents an interesting case study area for US–China comparison and core-activity benchmarking. Moreover, empirical testing could identify much more causal relationships and generate specific insights on the effects of Renminbi internationalization, digitalization, and geopolitical and social economic changes following the COVID-19 pandemic. While we focused on network effects and ecosystem construction, further research can examine how a platform identifies opportunities and develops its innovation, partnership, and marketing strategies.

9. Conclusion

Ant's platform expansion journey was representative of China's digital economy, constituting 38.6% of China's GDP in 2020 (less than 10% in the US and the UK). Ant leveraged Alipay's 900 million users to create a one-stop marketplace for financial products, including short- and long-term credit loans, insurance products, and wealth management offerings. Before the outbreak of the pandemic, Ant also capitalized on the Chinese tourists and her purchasing powers in Asia to expand the e-commerce and mobile payment markets, by investing and collaborating with domestic technology firms in the region.

In our paper, we also discussed the dilemmas between innovation, regulation, and monopolistic markets. First, a platform-based digital financial innovation can help improve competition and enhance consumer experiences and services. It can also provide inclusive financing to unbanked or underbanked groups. However, economies of scale, network externalities, and strong data control positions raise barriers to entry for newcomers through a monopolistic or oligopolistic market structure. Second, regulators have increasing concerns over the concentration of consumer data into limited hands, especially on issues related to data privacy, security, and protection. Hacking or security breaches can expose digital assets, such as customer data, resulting in vulnerabilities and threats including impact to national security. Third, network externalities and boundaries of a platform are blurred, and dynamic compared to the traditional banking businesses. For example, in the financial products trading facilitation business, shared responsibilities between platform owners and partner banks for credit assessments and operational risk management are not always clear due to the complexity of the financial products and how they are marketed.

Ant was not the only technology firm asked to restructure its digital financial platform business. In April 2021, JD Technology, a Fintech arm owned by JD.Com (a large e-commerce, warehouse, and logistics operator in China), withdrew its application for its IPO in Shanghai. Other technology giants including Tencent, ByteDance (owner of TikTok), Meituan (a food delivery platform), and DiDi (a transport provider similar to Uber) were also summoned by regulators for their "excessive innovation" in consumer financing activities and misuse of personal data. Before this wave of regulatory tightening, many of China's popular mobile apps offered consumer financing or loan products. The platform economy's rapid expansion through network effects from online distribution of financial products created new challenges for regulatory stress testing. In 2020, the Chinese government started a digital yuan pilot rollout program in several cities. This program could be an attempt to put citizen payment data back under sovereign control. However, without a supporting platform economy to engage with users, it is unlikely to see extensive usage. With the rapid expansion of the platform economy model, new regulations and data protection frameworks will have to be implemented. Ant's strategic pivot will certainly serve as a reference for other players and regulatory bodies to consider.

References

Armstrong, M., 2006, Competition in Two-sided Markets, *The RAND Journal of Economics* 37, 668–691.

Boudreau, K., and A. Hagiu, 2009, Platform Rules: Multi-sided Platforms as Regulators, in A. Gawer (editor), *Platforms, Markets and Innovation*, Edward Elgar Publishing, Northampton, MA, pp. 163–191.

Cennamo, C., and J. Santalo, 2013, Platform Competition: Strategic Trade-offs in Platform Markets, *Strategic Management Journal* 34(11), 1331–1350.

de las Heras Ballell, T. R., 2020, The Layers of Digital Financial Innovation: Charting a Regulatory Response, *Fordham Journal of Corporate & Financial Law* 25(2), 381–421.

Elia, G., V. Stefanelli, and G. B. Ferilli, 2022, Investigating the Role of Fintech in the Banking Industry: What do We Know?, *European Journal of Innovation Management*, doi:10.1108/EJIM-12-2021-0608.

Eisenmann, T. R., G. Parker, and M. van Alstyne, 2006, Strategies for Two-sided Markets, *Harvard Business Review* 84(10), 92–101.

Evans, D., 2003, The Antitrust Economics of Multi-sided Platform Markets, *Yale Journal on Regulation* 20(2), 325–382.

Farrell, J., and G. Saloner, 1985, Standardization, Compatibility, and Innovation, *The RAND Journal of Economics* 16(1), 70–83.

Ferrier, W., K. G. Smith, and C. M. Grimm, 1999, The Role of Competitive Action in Market Share Erosion and Industry Dethronement: A Study of Industry Leaders and Challengers, *Academy of Management Journal* 42(4), 372–388.

Gawer, A., and M. A. Cusumano, 2014, Industry Platforms and Ecosystem Innovation, *Journal of Product Innovation Management* 31, 417–433.

Huang, K. F., R. Dyerson, L. Y. Wu, and G. Harindranath, 2015, From Temporary Competitive Advantage to Sustainable Competitive Advantage, *British Journal of Management* 26(4), 617–636.

iResearch, 2020, China Third-party Payment Market Data Report (2020Q1 & 2020Q2e). Beijing: iResearch Inc.

Katz, M. L., and C. Shapiro, 1994, Systems Competition and Network Effects, *Journal of Economic Perspectives* 8, 93–99.

Katz, M. L., and C. Shapiro, 1985, Network Externalities, Competition, and Compatibility, *American Economic Review* 75(3), 424–440.

Kretschmer, T., A. Leiponen, M. Schilling, and G. Vasudeva, 2022, Platform Ecosystems as Meta-organizations: Implications for Platform Strategies, *Strategic Management Journal* 43(3), 405–424.

Li, F., 2021, Sustainable Competitive Advantages via Temporary Advantages: Insights from the Competition between American and Chinese Digital Platforms in China, *British Journal of Management* 33(4), 2009–2032.

Nucciarelli, A., F. Li, K. J. Fernandes, N. Goumagias, I. Cabras, S. Devlin, and P. Cowling, 2017, From Value Chains to Technological Platforms: The Effects of Crowdfunding in the Digital Game Industry, *Journal of Business Research* 78, 341–352.

Panico, C., and C. Cennamo, 2022, User Preferences and Strategic Interactions in Platform Ecosystems, *Strategic Management Journal* 43(3), 507–529.

Parker, G., and M. Van Alstyne, 2018, Innovation, Openness, and Platform Control, *Management Science* 64(7), 3015–3032.

Pon, B., T. Seppälä, and M. Kenney, 2014, Android and the Demise of Operating System-based Power: Firm Strategy and Platform Control in the Post-PC World, *Telecommunications Policy* 38(11), 979–991.

Rochet, J. C., and J. Tirole, 2003, Platform Competition in Two-sided Markets, *Journal of the European Economic Association* 1(4), 990–1029.

Rochet, J. C., and J. Tirole, 2006, Two-sided Markets: A Progress Report, *The RAND Journal of Economics* 37(3), 645–667.

Trabucchi, D., and T. Buganza, 2021, Landlords with No Lands: A Systematic Literature Review on Hybrid Multi-sided Platforms and Platform Thinking, *European Journal of Innovation Management* 25(6), 64–96.

Tiwana, A., B. Konsynski, and A. Bush, 2010, Platform Evolution: Coevolution of Platform Architecture, Governance, and Environmental Dynamics, *Information Systems Research* 21(4), 675–687.

Yin, R. K., 1994, *Case Study Research Design and Methods: Applied Social Research and Methods Series*, 2nd edition, Sage Publications, Inc., Thousand Oaks, CA.

Zeng, J., and K. W. Glaister, 2016, Competitive Dynamics between Multinational Enterprises and Local Internet Platform Companies in the Virtual Market in China, *British Journal of Management* 27(3), 479–496.

Zhu, F., 2019, Friends or Foes? Examining Platform Owners' Entry into Complementors' Spaces, *Journal of Economics & Management Strategy* 28(1), 23–28.

Privacy and New Types of Money

Kenneth Bok

Blocks.sg, Singapore

The future of money is set to change dramatically in the next few years, with blockchain taking center stage in transforming the ledger in the banking system at both the commercial bank layer and the central bank layer. Additionally, the emergence of stablecoins has highlighted the benefits of open finance through the use of blockchain. New types of money do not necessarily require the use of a blockchain, but a majority do involve blockchain technology.

However, the issue of privacy has been increasingly important given the sensitivity of financial transactions. Privacy is the right to keep personal information secret or known only to a trusted group of people (Bank for International Settlements, 2023).

The Bank of Canada classifies privacy into three types (Bank for International Settlements, 2023):

1. **Confidential**: Only trusted parties can see personal information.
2. **Pseudoanonymous**: Public addresses are used, and parties can only be identified if a link between a public address and a real-world identity is known. This is typical for transactions on platforms like Bitcoin or Ethereum.
3. **Anonymous**: Parties cannot be identified, such as in cash payments.

The policy trade-offs for regulators and central banks for this issue revolve around privacy and the need to maintain financial security by preventing money laundering, terrorist financing (AML/CFT), tax evasion, and other criminal activities. In public discourse, CBDCs in particular have raised significant concerns about privacy, especially in the US and EU.

Let's examine the differences between these three new types of money — CBDCs, tokenized deposits, and stablecoins — and how privacy is maintained in each of these solutions.

Some solutions around privacy and CBDCs include "managed anonymity," as implemented in the e-CNY system (Mu, 2022). In the e-CNY system, users can maintain anonymity for small-value transactions, similar to cash transactions. Higher transaction limits are allowed with higher KYC levels, in line with "anonymity for small amounts, traceability for large amounts in accordance with the law." For example, a level four wallet, which only requires a phone number to open, has a single transaction limit of CNY 2,000 (USD 276). A level one wallet, which requires an additional ID check, linkage to a bank account, and a physical visit to a bank branch, has an unlimited transaction limit.[1] The e-CNY also adopts a two-tiered system, with the PBC supplying e-CNY to authorized operators such as commercial banks. Personal information is collected and stored by authorized operators, while the PBC only processes inter-institutional transaction information and does not hold personal information.

Project Tourbillon, developed by the BIS Innovation Hub Swiss Centre, explores the privacy, security, and scalability of CBDCs. At the core of these requirements is cryptography, and with quantum computing on the horizon, the project tested quantum-blind signatures — a cryptographic technique ensuring anonymity. In Project Tourbillon, payer anonymity is introduced, meaning consumers paying merchants do not disclose personal information to merchants, banks, or central banks. The identity of the merchant is known confidentially to the merchant bank. While the central bank does not access personal payment data, it can monitor CBDC circulation at an aggregated level (Bank for International Settlements, 2023).

Tokenized deposit projects, compared to CBDCs, are still in their infancy. However, we can safely assume that production-grade blockchain solutions for tokenized deposits will prioritize privacy as a key feature. Recently, at the Singapore FinTech Festival, Umar Farooq, CEO of Onyx by JP Morgan, weighed in on the type of blockchain that would be used by banks, stating that "sending $100 million to another bank on a public blockchain where no one is accountable is not feasible."[2] It was also at this panel that the Global Layer One initiative was announced. Led by MAS, in collaboration with other financial institutions such as BNY Mellon, DBS, JP Morgan, and MUFG, GL1 looks to explore the design of

---

[1] https://www.linkedin.com/posts/jamiel_the-e-cny-has-a-4-tier-kyc-scale-the-lowest-activity-6890320280573874177-vuUB/.

[2] https://www.youtube.com/watch?v=hHLXiAfGTRE&ab_channel=SingaporeFinTechFestival.

"an open, digital infrastructure that will host tokenized financial assets and applications … while meeting relevant regulatory requirements and guidelines."[3]

Lastly, with stablecoins, full anonymity is not achieved. Currently, USDC and USDT use public Ethereum (and other similar blockchains), which offers only pseudo-anonymity. If an address is linked to a real-world identity, it becomes possible to trace the movement of funds indefinitely on the blockchain, which is, of course, transparent.

The trade-offs between these three new types of money are between connectivity, control, and privacy. It is challenging to maintain true anonymity in the "Wild West" of blockchain, where connectivity is tremendous and nearly impossible to beat due to the seamless and innovative interconnectivity. As we move into more regulated types of banking, privacy will become much more of a hard requirement. Solutions like zero-knowledge proofs could be utilized in these systems to enhance privacy.

Both Project Tourbillon and the e-CNY system emphasize a balance between privacy and regulatory compliance by ensuring payer anonymity while still enabling necessary oversight. Both systems rely on authorized intermediaries to manage personal information and ensure compliance with AML/CFT requirements, thereby protecting user privacy while maintaining financial security. This approach mirrors the current monetary system, where intermediaries play a crucial role in safeguarding privacy while facilitating regulatory compliance.

References

Bank for International Settlements (BIS). (2023). Project Tourbillon. https://www.bis.org/publ/othp80.htm.

Mu, C. (2022). Balancing Privacy and Security: Theory and Practice of the E-CNY's Managed Anonymity. http://www.pbc.gov.cn/en/3935690/3935759/4696666/2022110110364344083.pdf.

[3] https://www.mas.gov.sg/news/media-releases/2023/mas-partners-financial-industry-to-expand-asset-tokenisation-initiatives#1.

Beyond Trustlessness: Unveiling Counterparty Risks in DeFi

Luc Froehlich

Pontoon Capital, Hong Kong, China

1. How Credit Risk Analysis Can Propel DeFi into a New Era of Security and Trust

Decentralized finance (DeFi) offers novel and inclusive ways to participate in financial services. It promises to replace the opaque operations of traditional finance (TradFi) with transparency and verifiable processes. The technology, particularly a combination of smart contracts operating on blockchain, appears to remove the need for trust and reliance on centrally controlled entities.

2. The Promise and Perils of DeFi

You would be excused if you believe that DeFi removes counterparty risk thanks to atomic swaps, i.e., simultaneous wallet-to-wallet exchanges of two digital assets. You might even fall for a false logic: TradFi relies on trust to mitigate counterparty risk; DeFi no longer requires trust; ergo, DeFi eliminates counterparty risk. However, the reality is more nuanced. Technological feats alone do not eliminate risk, and risk management cannot stop with smart contract audits. Our desire to remove the need for trust from financial services might have blinded us to the fact that counterparty risk is omnipresent in the current journey of a DeFi user.

3. Understanding Counterparty Risk in DeFi

Counterparty risk commonly refers to the likelihood that one of the parties in a financial transaction defaults on its obligations and the potential magnitude of the ensuing damage for the other party. This default could be a failure to repay a loan (credit risk) or to settle a transaction (settlement risk). In DeFi, over-collateralization is typically used to mitigate counterparty risk, although it can provide a false sense of security as systemic risks are easily underestimated. Where TradFi mitigates counterparty risk through legal agreements and regulations, DeFi sets up self-executing rules.

Defining DeFi proves more challenging, and the space is best captured using a spectrum from true DeFi to hybrid to plain "fake" DeFi. The latter includes platforms offering to connect users with their wallets but leaving asset management in the hands of mere humans. Correct categorization is critical as each bucket exposes users to widely different levels of counterparty risk.

4. Navigating the DeFi Landscape: A Pragmatic User's Journey

We will take three snapshots in a DeFi user's journey to unveil the existence of counterparty risk in each phase. But before even connecting their wallet, users need to acknowledge the challenges attached to permissionless systems. DeFi lowers barriers of entry to financial services not only for users but also for protocol operators and token issuers. This exposes end users to project-related risks, such as rug pulls and the possibility of interacting with wallets involved in suspicious or illicit activities. While retail users might swallow this pill, institutions will stay far away from such reputational risks.

Storing: Once users acquire digital assets, they must be safely stored. Keeping them with a third-party custodian reduces control over the assets, introducing custodian risk. Storing assets by oneself adds the burden of keeping them safe and implies relying on wallet providers to stay in business and regularly update their software for security. Additionally, managing private key access can add to counterparty risk if users trust a third party to maintain part of their key or keep their recovery seed.

Interacting: DeFi users can perform various transactions, typically linked to trading, lending, and borrowing. Decentralized exchanges and lending platforms are typically operated through DAOs. However, decentralization does not necessarily eliminate counterparty risk. Users must investigate the governance mechanisms of each DAO to understand their voting mechanisms and the concentration of decision-making power. A high concentration of governance tokens in a few hands and low participation rates can erode decentralization, replacing it with counterparty risk.

Exiting: Users seeking a safe haven would move from volatile cryptocurrencies to stablecoins. This strategy allows quick re-engagement with DeFi platforms while minimizing friction and costs. However, this step exposes users to the risk of stablecoins maintaining their peg, typically to fiat currencies. Negative headlines or general distrust can cause a stablecoin's peg to deviate, a textbook example of counterparty risk. This issue goes beyond counterparty risk, requiring consideration of systemic risk, as illustrated by the temporary de-pegging of stablecoins due to the failure of US regional banks in 2023.

5. Building a Safer DeFi: The Role of Credit Analysis

The above-mentioned examples demonstrate that trustlessness has its limitations. Ironically, the challenge points toward its solution: credit. The term "credit" originates from the Latin "credere," meaning "to trust." Trust does not have to be blind, and credit analysis might be the way forward for DeFi. So far, the digital assets space has mostly shunned credit work, partly because very few participants have professional credit backgrounds. The additional challenge is to refrain from reintroducing centralization by concentrating credit work on a single entity. The idea remains that by tagging entities controlling critical steps in DeFi, users would benefit from indications about the creditworthiness of their counterparties instead of relying on the elusive trustlessness of the technology.

NFTs: Hype, Hope, or Here to Stay?

Sandy Oh

Singapore Management University, Singapore

Are NFTs hype, hope, or here to stay? Before addressing the question, it is useful to establish a common understanding of what NFTs are by breaking down the concepts of "non-fungibility" and "token." Assets like the US dollar and crypto-currencies like BTC and ETH are considered fungible and users treat them as interchangeable. When we are presented with two USD 1 dollar notes, we treat them as identical and substitutable. In contrast, NFTs are unique and different, hence users regard them as non-interchangeable and non-fungible. The "token" in an NFT is a digital token on a blockchain tied to metadata about the asset it represents. The token ID is the NFT's defining feature; it is a "unique 1-of-1 barcode that distinguishes the NFT from any other token on the blockchain it is on."[1] For the very first time, proof of ownership can be represented via tokens and recorded immutably and transparently on the blockchain. Furthermore, the token ID is tied to the owner's blockchain address, which means the NFT is entirely controlled by the owner. This is significant as digital assets in the Web2 world are typically owned and controlled by the centralized platforms on which they are created. Currently, when we buy digital items, like e-books or digital music, we are simply acquiring a license to use them. We don't own the e-book or the music file and cannot lend or pass them on. NFTs challenge this model by allowing the owners to own and transfer the assets at their discretion.

It is crucial to distinguish between NFTs' technical features as blockchain-based, tokenized records that guarantee the uniqueness of an asset and the applications of NFTs. Recognizing the distinction allows for a more sober assessment and appreciation of their potential versus the hype. As the examples will show,

[1] *Source*: https://blog.chain.link/real-world-asset-nft/. (Accessed on 11 June 2024).

experimentation with NFTs began as early as 2013 with Bitcoin-based colored coins. Earlier experiments did not attract much fanfare, and it was not until 2021 that NFTs captured mainstream consciousness with media coverage of overnight millionaires, celebrity endorsements, and institutional investments. Monthly sales of NFTs in August 2021 and January 2022 ballooned to the region of USD 5.5 to 6 billion. This figure has since dropped to below USD 200,000 in June 2024.[2] Much of the hype and trading were in Profile Picture (PFP) NFTs and Art NFTs. PFP NFTs are typically collections of randomly generated unique images of punks, animals, and avatars, and the most well-known examples are CryptoPunks and Bored Ape Yacht Club. The floor price of a Bored Ape went from 0.08 ETH (when it was created in 2021) to a peak of nearly 150 ETH (in 2022) to 12 ETH (in 2024).[3] Digital art has been around since computers were invented in the 1970s. However, it was NFT technology that enabled artists and collectors to own and trade them. This facilitated many breakout NFT artists, one example being Tyler Hobbs. The floor price of his Fidenza collection traded to a peak of around 350 ETH (in 2021) before settling at 30 ETH (in 2024). Both examples show that despite their massive drop in prices, there is still value attributed to these NFTs. They are, however, exceptions to the rule. Most other NFT projects are now worth next to nothing. With the benefit of hindsight, was this all just hype?

Writing off NFTs because their price bubble has burst is analogous to writing off the internet after the dotcom bubble burst (in 1999) or blockchain after the ICO bubble (2017). It is repeating the mistake of conflating prices and extreme irrationality with NFTs' impact on cultural evolution and real technological innovation. For one, communities that are formed around surviving and successful PFP projects are still thriving. In secular societies where individuals are seeking new and alternative ways to find meaning and identity, some of these NFT communities have become vibrant hubs of interaction and belonging. The Discord channels of thriving PFP NFT projects, e.g., Pudgy Penguins, Doodles, and Dour Darcels, still show significant membership numbers and active, recent online and offline engagement.

On the tech side, the first wave has demonstrated NFTs' strong use case in the digital landscape for digital art, PFPs, collectibles, music, gaming, fashion, and metaverse assets. The next wave we are witnessing now is NFTs' use case in Real-World Assets (RWAs). RWAs cover a whole spectrum from investment assets, e.g., stocks, bonds, funds, and real estate, to alternative assets, e.g., physical

[2] *Source*: https://www.cryptoslam.io/nftglobal?headerPeriod=all&timeFrame=month. (Accessed on 10 June 2024)

[3] *Source*: https://www.coingecko.com/en/nft/bored-ape-yacht-club. (Accessed on 10 June 2024).

collectibles like watches, fine wines, high-end clothes, shoes, and trading cards.[4,5,6] In this case, NFTs' technical features can be optimized to represent physical non-fungible RWAs. Real estate is generally non-fungible as each property has unique attributes and locations. Hence, NFTs can be used if the goal is to tokenize and trade the property as a whole.[7,8] The potential for NFT application in RWA is tremendous and we are starting to see its application in various asset classes.

There have also been new developments in NFTs' technical abilities to broaden their usefulness. In the paper "From NFT 1.0 to NFT 2.0: A Review of the Evolution of Non-Fungible Tokens" by Guidi and Michienzi (2023), they define NFT 1.0 as the era of "static NFTs" whereby the metadata are fixed and unchangeable when the token is created. This works well for artwork and collectibles but less so in use cases where the metadata need to be updated. NFT 2.0, also known as "dynamic NFTs" or dNFTs, allows its metadata to be changed from interaction with external data and systems. This feature widens the scope of NFT applications tremendously. For example, in sports, a dynamic NFT can be tied to one specific player and updated according to the player's performance, as in NBA's Association NFTs.[9] In medical devices, Gebreab *et al.* (2023) propose using dynamic NFTs to manage refurbished medical devices to create a transparent and verifiable record of the refurbishment process to ensure the safety and quality of the devices. In healthcare and medical research, Yaghy *et al.* (2023) propose using NFTs to tokenize health data, so that individuals can control and monetize their data if they choose to. They further posit that NFTs can be used to optimize the stem cell transplant process by enabling real-time inventory management and matching between donor and transplant centers.

At their core, NFTs simply facilitate the tokenization of all types of data and assets. The Bank of International Settlements, an institution not known for hyperbole, recently laid out its vision of a future financial system that "leverages innovative technologies such as tokenisation and unified ledgers" (Carstens and Nilekani, 2024). If we agree with this view that the world is moving toward a tokenized economy, then NFTs will increasingly play a bigger role. NFTs have already demonstrated their use cases for verifiable ownership in digital assets, as

[4] *Source*: https://courtyard.io/about. (Accessed on 11 June 2024).

[5] *Source*: https://www.iyk.app/. (Accessed on 11 June 2024)

[6] *Source*: https://arx.org/. (Accessed on 11 June 2024).

[7] *Source*: https://www.entrepreneur.com/business-news/the-first-nft-home-just-sold-for-175000/437522. (Accessed on 11 June 2024).

[8] *Source*: https://onchain.roofstock.com/properties. (Accessed on 11 June 2024).

[9] *Source*: https://opensea.io/collection/the-association-nft. (Accessed on 11 June 2024).

well as being a new avenue for creators and brands in building direct and stronger relationships with their supporters. Research and development show that the possibilities for NFTs truly depend on human creativity and imagination. As such, NFTs will continue to evolve and are here to stay.

References

Carstens, A. and Nilekani, N. 2024. Finternet: The Financial System for the Future. *Working Paper.* https://www.bis.org/publ/work1178.htm.

Gebreab, S., Salah, K., Jayaraman, R., and Zemerly, J. 2023. Trusted traceability and certification of refurbished medical devices using dynamic composable NFTs. *IEEE Xplore*. https://ieeexplore.ieee.org/document/10080959.

Guidi, B. and Michienzi, A. 2023. From NFT 1.o to NFT 2.0: A review of the evolution of non-fungible tokens. *Future Internet*. https://www.mdpi.com/1999-5903/15/6/189.

Yaghy, A., Alberto, N., Alberto I., Bermea R., Ristovska L., Yaghy M., Hoyek S., Patel N., and Celi, L. 2023. The potential use of non-fungible tokens (NFTs) in healthcare and medical research. *PLOS Digit Health*. https://www.ncbi.nlm.nih.gov/pmc/articles/PMC10374113/.

In the Finternet, Survival of the Fittest

Alvin Chia

Northern Trust, Singapore

Ever since Agustin Carstens, general manager of the Bank of International Settlement, and Nandan Nilekani, tech entrepreneur, published[1] their concept of the "Finternet" in April 2024, observers have been fascinated with their vision of a digital ecosystem to unite the financial world.

Much like how people browse, order, and pay across thousands of connected sites on the web, the Finternet in its ideal state will link the world's scattered financial entities to facilitate seamless back-end transactions.

It may be helpful to picture this proposition as a blockchain layer overlaid on financial markets, akin to what Society for Worldwide Interbank Financial Telecommunication (SWIFT's) network brought to the traditional financial markets in the 1970s, when it enabled banking systems to communicate in a seamless and effective way across organizations. The goal is to maximize efficiency and eradicate delays, red tape, and other symptoms of ineffective money handling.

The latest in a series of tectonic shifts decentralizing finance, the Finternet, if realized, will likely claim the tasks now undertaken by middlemen, who facilitate the process of connecting buyers and sellers across jurisdictions and asset classes.

This potential disruption puts forth the following question: In a model with atomic settlement, what will happen to the thousands of financial intermediaries on which the current system runs?

[1] https://www.bis.org/publ/work1178.htm.

1. Not so Fast

The simple and perhaps unwelcomed prediction is that yes, firms might be disrupted by the latest wave of innovation.

Some are more at risk than others. Banks are likely to retain their value as an anchor within the ecosystem, but function-specific fintech firms, those built to resolve or alleviate a specific pain point, could take a hit.

Clearing and settlement houses might see displacement from blockchain technology enabled by the automation of smart contracts. Meanwhile, firms that facilitate market-making — such as Web 3.0-centric exchanges — would require further stress testing before gaining wider adoption.

But there is time to adjust. The scale and scope of jurisdictional collaboration required to realize stringent, globally unified financial regulation, and the likely need for a supranational organization to lead the charge mean the Finternet could take a decade or more to materialize.

When it does unfold, its growth path could likely echo the trajectory of other major technological innovations. First, the initial wave, where regulators, exchanges, banks, and fintech firms — all seeking to build the overarching blockchain that connects the Finternet — crowd the space with trials.

Next, saturation. Directions diverge as companies pursue niches. Finally, attrition and consolidation, concluding in a potential oligopoly.

This first step is already unfolding, given recent multi-party pilots such as Canton Network's interoperable blockchain for institutional assets that Northern Trust participated in[2]; Project Agorá's tokenized cross-border payments[3]; and Marketnode's DLT-powered, fixed-income infrastructure.[4]

By many measures, a mature Finternet is great news for intermediaries, who stand to reap efficiency rewards. Fewer administrative hoops and higher institutional connectivity mean quicker trades at lower rates, translating to faster time to market and better value for clients.

The key is staying relevant as the paradigm shifts.

2. Doubling Down on Value

Traditionally, the value of intermediaries lies in enhancing market liquidity by facilitating faster asset movement. But with the Finternet, role consolidation is

[2] https://www.canton.network/pilot-press-release?utm_source=Linkedin&amp.

[3] https://www.bis.org/press/p240403.htm.

[4] https://www.marketnode.com/media-centre/sgx-temasek.

likely as process workflows shrink to fewer steps and clients continue the ongoing process of scaling down on providers.

To thrive in this new environment, intermediaries must clarify their value proposition and transform quickly to avoid being switched out for rivals who offer better connectivity, more robust analytics, or efficiency.

Chief among these is rooting out inefficiencies and learning to operate in a trustless world of seamless activity. For one, even with a global unified ledger, some identity verification will likely still be required — possibly a simplified version that works across systems (Project Guardian in Singapore made trust anchor a key focus area of the initiative[5]). Whatever the case, intermediaries' infrastructure must be able to handle digital credentialing and trustless identity tools.

More importantly, the continued relevance of intermediaries lies in providing value-added services that blockchain functionality cannot: market knowledge, regulatory expertise, and insight into local contexts and licensing models.

One potential focus area is security. In theory, the Finternet could be compliant by design, with whitelisting as a prerequisite. Once verified, users can pursue investment activities, perhaps aided by service providers. However, the reality is that new technologies expose us to emerging risks that cannot yet be conceptualized — think blockchain's susceptibility to tech loopholes resulting in lost assets, or bad actors hacking into wallets and intercepting and redirecting funds.

In such an ecosystem, intermediaries function as a trusted third party, helping clients navigate trading and holding risks. Global custodians such as Northern Trust play roles in supporting investment activity across markets and safekeeping institutional assets.

A second focus is convenience. The Finternet's frictionless state of finance will likely be achieved through tokenization, requiring fluency in the medium. And though the Finternet promises seamless transactions, the same cannot be said for user experience. Here, intermediaries can undertake the task of navigating evolving systems.

Though decentralized finance is hardly a new concept, it is a vision more real today than ever before, given new technologies. The Finternet is the latest expression of this ideal state, and these are its early days, with opportunities to navigate to positions of future prominence.

When mature, there will potentially be nothing like the Finternet in the market. Intermediaries simply need to survive the sea change to be there to see it.

---

[5] https://www.mas.gov.sg/schemes-and-initiatives/project-guardian.

Services SE Netherlands Branch, Viñoly 7th floor, Claude Debussylaan 18 A, 1082 MD Amsterdam; Northern Trust Global Services SE Abu Dhabi Branch, registration Number 000000519 licenced by ADGM under FSRA #160018; Northern Trust Global Services SE Norway Branch, org. no. 925 952 567 (Foretaksregisteret), address Third Floor, Haakon VIIs gate 6 0161 Oslo, is a Norwegian branch of Northern Trust Global Services SE supervised by Finanstilsynet. Northern Trust Global Services SE Leudelange, Luxembourg, Zweigniederlassung Basel is a branch of Northern Trust Global Services SE. The Branch has its registered office at Grosspeter Tower, Grosspeteranlage 29, 4052 Basel, Switzerland, and is authorised and regulated by the Swiss Financial Market Supervisory Authority FINMA. The Northern Trust Company Saudi Arabia, PO Box 7508, Level 20, Kingdom Tower, Al Urubah Road, Olaya District, Riyadh, Kingdom of Saudi Arabia 11214-9597, a Saudi Joint Stock Company – capital 52 million SAR. Regulated and Authorised by the Capital Market Authority License #12163-26 CR 1010366439. Northern Trust (Guernsey) Limited (2651)/Northern Trust Fiduciary Services (Guernsey) Limited (29806)/Northern Trust International Fund Administration Services (Guernsey) Limited (15532) are licensed by the Guernsey Financial Services Commission. Registered Office: Trafalgar Court, Les Banques, St Peter Port, Guernsey GY1 3DA. Northern Trust International Fund Administration Services (Ireland) Limited (160579)/Northern Trust Fiduciary Services (Ireland) Limited (161386), Registered Office: Georges Court, 54-62 Townsend Street, Dublin 2, D02 R156, Ireland.

www.ingramcontent.com/pod-product-compliance
Lightning Source LLC
LaVergne TN
LVHW081933200926
848484LV00009B/2419